CORPORATE INTERIORS
No.2

Retail Reporting Corporation
302 Fifth Avenue
New York, NY 10001

Distributors to the trade in the United States and Canada
Watson-Guptill
1515 Broadway
New York, NY 10036

Distributors outside the United States and Canada
Hearst Books International
1350 Avenue of the Americas
New York, NY 10019

Library of Congress Cataloging in Publication Data:
Corporate Interiors

Printed in Hong Kong
ISBN 0-934590-99-0

Book Design: Harish Patel Design Associates, New York

CORPORATE INTERIORS

No.2

Stanley Abercrombie, FAIA, Hon. FASID, Hon. IIDA

Retail Reporting Corporation, New York

CONTENTS

Introduction

In 1996, Corporate Interiors was nothing more than a gleam in the eye of Lester Dundes, the publisher emeritus of Interior Design magazine. But Lester has a way of translating gleams into action. By the middle of 1977, the first edition of the book was published, presenting the work of 33 interior design firms that had been invited to participate. It had been Lester's contention that, while bookstores, magazine stands, and even newspapers are packed with information about residential interior design, those who want information about interior design for offices and other sorts of commercial design have little to choose from. The first book's success proves Lester was right.

So right that, roughly a year later, we are pleased to present this second edition, and there is every indication that a series of annual editions will follow. For those who have seen book number one, is there any need for book number two? How do the editions differ? These questions are similar to asking if, having seen one issue of a magazine, is there any point in seeing another. Sometimes, of course, the answer is no. But not in this case. The first book presented, as we said, the work of 33 leading firms. Each was given an identifying opening page and seven additional pages in which to show its work, and each made its own choices about which installations it most wanted to show. Some firms concentrated on only a couple of examples, showing them in detail, while others presented a greater variety. In addition, I attempted to briefly summarize the current practice of so-called "contract design," and designer/educator Michael D. Tatus, IIDA, contributed a valuable guide to the process of choosing a design firm.

This second edition is both bigger and different. The number of firms accepting Lester Dundes's invitation to participate has grown to 45. Some of them are repeats from the first year's group, some are new, but even those who are repeats have chosen to display new and different work. And this year, in explanation of a trend that is obvious in many of the examples shown, there is an essay on "What Alternative Officing (AO) Really Means" by Marilyn Zelinsky.

The result, we think, presents in one volume an unmatched review of the best work being done today in the field of corporate design. Perhaps the only reading experience that could offer as much information is a year's subscription to Interior Design, now being skillfully edited by Mayer Rus. But that magazine, while read by some laymen, is written for the design professional. This book, while read by some designers, is written for the potential consumer of design services--the corporate executive who wants a crash course in what's available, what services to expect from design firms, who those design firms are and where they're located, and what the most skillfully designed offices of today really look like. In the very back of the book, this information is supplemented by advertisements that show some of the components of corporate interior design now on the market.

It should be noted that, while only a small group of respected design firms was invited to take part, the selection of work is their own. There was no design jury choosing its favorites and enforcing its taste. A particular point is therefore missing in this collection, but we believe this lace is compensated for by the resultant multiplicity of viewpoints. For most readers, this catholicity is more valuable--and presents a more realistic picture of actual design practice today--than a more carefully edited selection.

Having design firms select their own material also tells us rather clearly what those firms consider to be important. In seven pages, no firm can display more than a small fraction of its output. Working within these limitations, our 45 firms can show us only the work of which they are most proud. Some focus on the most lavish commissions, some on accomplishments within tight budgets. Some spotlight large jobs, some small. Some attempt to present the big picture with overall images, some concentrate on telling details. Their choices among examples of their own work are as informative as the work itself. Readers are reminded, however, that choices have had to be made, and that the complete story of any design firm's capabilities can only be known on the basis of greater exposure and personal interviews.

This book is not, therefore, intended as a final arbiter in the process of selecting a design firm, but rather as a helpful guide to the beginning of that process. We hope you will find it fulfills that intention.

Stanley Abercrombie, FAIA, Hon. FASID, Hon. IIDA

Ai

1445 New York Avenue, NW

Suite 400

Washington DC 20005

202.734.1020

202.737.0879 (Fax)

Ai

**America Online Headquarters
Creative Center One
Dulles, Virginia**

Right: *Reception and visitor waiting area.* ***Below:*** *The facility's library.* ***Phototgraphy:*** *Jeff Goldberg, ESTO.*

Right: *View from the newly extended mezzanine level.*
Below, right: *The cafeteria and coffee bar and their window wall.*

Ai converted a former airplane parts warehouse for British Aerospace into this facility for America Online. In only six months the existing 123,000 square feet were increased to 183,000 by the extension of a mezzanine level within the 30-ft.-high warehouse. New windows were opened into the largely blank concrete facade, and new skylights through the roof created a number of two-story-high internal atria within the massive floor plate. In addition, new project-ing wings pads contain conference rooms jutting into the landscape. The thoroughly renovated building now houses 640 America Online employees, and facilities include a two-level dining area and a cafeteria, training/conferencing center, a computer center, a library, a coffee bar, a company store, game rooms, and various other nontraditional spaces where, it is expected, creative endeavors will be fostered. Ai's work began with evaluation of the former warehouse and extended to architecture, interior design, and the engineering of the mechanical, electrical, and plumbing systems. The project earned Ai a Best Interior Award of Excellence from the Northern Virginia chapter of the National Association of Industrial and Office Properties.

Ai

Connie Lee
Corporate Offices
Washington, DC

Winner of awards from the Washington Building Congress, the American Woodwork Institute, and the Illuminating Engineering Society of America, these offices for an insurance corporation occupy 25,000 square feet in the new office building adjoining Washington's historic Warner Theater. The processional route through the office from elevator lobby to executive areas employs an interesting series of spatial compressions and expansions. Weaving through these spaces is a screen made of solid cherry framing imported japanese "shoji" glass. These screens serve as walls that in places slide and pivot to convert spaces for multiple usages, provide light and conceal credenzas. Other materials employed are cherry veneer wall panels, maple flooring, brushed bronze, black granite, drywall ceilings, and natural silk wallcoverings. The space houses 72 Connie Lee employees.

Above: *The client's logo at the entrance.*
Left: *Workstation grouping with lighting niche.*

Ai

The Advisory Board Company
Headquarters
Washington, DC

The Advisory Board Company, a publishing firm, retained Ai to provide interior architectural design services for the consolidation of its eight Capitol Hill offices and their relocation to the Watergate complex in northwest Washington. In these new quarters, the company's 200 employees occupy a total of 100,000 square feet spread over three floors. Connecting these levels and serving as a dramatic focal point is a spiral stair. As a company involved in the collection and dissemination of information, The Advisory Board wanted a space that would evoke an era of ideas and inspire not only its staff but also its visitors and clientele. To that end, the stair, strategically located rotundas and square pavilions, and elements throughout the installation are classically inspired and detailed. Materials and colors are clean, light, and simple, with the addition of stone and stucco complementing the classical references.

Ai

**Federal Home Loan Mortgage Corporation
Headquarters Phase III
McLean, Virginia**

The Federal Home Loan Mortgage Corporation (familiarly known as "Freddie Mac") is an important financial services organization. To consolidate from a number of scattered locations and to accommodate continued growth, it selected McLean, Virginia, for its headquarters campus. Three buildings, totaling 875,000 square feet, have been built to date on the site, which has been master planned for 1.2 million square feet. The Phase III building, consisting of 190,000 square feet on four floors, houses the 660 employees of Freddie Mac's Information Services Division and offers private and general office space, a cafeteria, a conference center, and telecommunications facilities. All have been designed in accordance with the Freddie Mac image: stable, yet progressive. For all three phases of the Freddie Mac headquarters construction, Ai has provided a full range of interior architecture services.

Ai

Student Loan Marketing Association
Consolidation Project
Reston, Virginia

The Student Loan Marketing Association (or "Sallie Mae") plans a three-phase, 850,000-square- foot consolidation project in Northern Virginia. This first phase is a nine-floor, 450,000-square-foot building for the association's Loan Servicing Center, Data Center, and administrative functions, branches that comprise a total of almost 1300 employees. Throughout the project, for which Ai provided full-range interior architecture and mechanical/electrical/plumbing engineering services, the design firm worked in close collaboration with the base building architect. Due to its rapidly changing work environment, Sallie Mae's primary goal in the facility was flexibility, and Ai conducted studies of column bays and workstation sizes as a prelude to developing floor plate layouts with the maximum accommodation of change. The typical floor area is 80 percent open, with enclosed offices along the interior core, allowing daylight and extensive landscape views into perimeter work areas.

AREA

550 South Hope Street

18th Floor

Los Angeles

California 90071

213.623.8909

213.623.4275 (Fax)

area30@aol.com

Endeavor
Beverly Hills, California

Right: Discreet logo at reception desk.
Below: Workstations and custom cabinetry for agents' assistants.
Photography: Jon Miller/Hedrich-Blessing.

Far left: Detail of cabinetry grid with built-in uplighting.
Left: Waiting room with reception area and conference room beyond.

Winner of a top 1997 award from the design competition co-sponsored by Interior Design magazine and the International Interior Design Association, this 15,000-square-foot office houses a four-year-old talent agency. The site itself was a challenge: the tenth floor of a determinedly nonrectangular office building with an ameboid plan. Also challenging was the young agency's need for instant image. While more established competitors impressed visitors with art collections, Endeavor decided to compete in other ways; the art here was to be the interior design itself. Within a composition of curved forms, relating to the building design and referring also to early Hollywood, Area has employed a materials palette of three kinds of limestone, two species of burl wood veneers, and white pearlescent paint. All components are unendangered, non-toxic, and environmentally safe.

19

AREA

3 Arts Entertainment
Beverly Hills, California

"It's the first time," says 3 Arts partner Erwin Stoff, "I have really enjoyed working in an office environment." Cause of that enjoyment is the AREA design of 8,300 square feet for the

26 employees of 3 Arts, a talent management company specializing in television and motion picture production. The designers took advantage of the concrete structure of the 30-year-old Beverly Hills commercial space by exposing and uplighting slabs and beams in all public spaces. The building architecture's three-foot fenestration module has also been employed throughout, expressed in vertical aluminum blades and in sandblasted glass panels that admit light but provide visual privacy. Other materials include figured European white ash, limestone, multicolor water-based wall coatings, and three-dimensional wall sculptures by Guy Dill. Kudos include awards from DuPont (for carpet treatment using colors of the 3 Arts logo) and from Interiors magazine.

Above: Conference room with banquette. **Below:** Reception/waiting area with exposed concrete ceiling and beams.

AREA

**Ziffren,
Brittenham,
Branca &
Fischer
Los Angeles,
California**

Right: Stair connecting the two attorney floors.
Below and opposite: Two views of a lounge/waiting area.
Photography: Jon Miller/Hedrich-Blessing.

The client firm is the preeminent entertainment law firm in the Los Angeles area. It required space for its 75 employees, an image that would defy the Hollywood stereotypes and please its elite client list, and a new look into which its existing art and furnishings could be integrated. The resultant installation occupies 35,000 square feet on five floors, the upper two of which are devoted to attorneys' offices and are linked by an internal stair. There is also a paralegal floor, a service floor with employee lounge, and a conference center. Common-grade figured American cherry was chosen for its characterful variations as the main wood throughout, with inlays and supporting pieces made of English yew, East Indian laurel, makore, and wenge.

Above and above, right: *Top and bottom of the stair connecting 4th and 5th floors.* **Right:** *Secretarial work-stations. Sculptured figures are from Kenya.*

Flooring is of Brazilian cherry and olive-green carpeting. Other colorings are multiple shades of green accented with red. Indirect lighting is built in, and wood-framed glazing near the ceiling makes possible a flow of light from office areas to corridor spaces. In addition to the office design, AREA provided prelease space analysis, space planning, construction management, and the specification of furniture and accessories.

ASD

50 Hurt Plaza
Suite 500
Atlanta
Georgia 30303
404.688.3318
404.688.2255 (Fax)

8614 Westwood Center Drive
Suite 110
Vienna
Virginia 22182
703.761.4188
703.893.5461 (Fax)

707 North Franklin Street
Suite 200
Tampa
Florida 33602
813.223.2293
813.223.2433 (Fax)

1120 Chester Avenue
Suite 370
Cleveland
Ohio 44114
216.241.3500
216.861.4045 (Fax)

ASD

Alumax
Atlanta, Georgia

Right: *Executive assistant's office.*
Below: *Reception area enlivened with an Alumax racecar.*
Photography: *Rion Rizzo.*

Not many firms have a racecar mounted on their reception area wall, but not many firms are in the business of aluminum distribution. And the racecar here is not the only dramatic feature, for behind the receptionist's custom-designed circular desk, a sculptural stair of wood and glass rises through all four levels of the office. Occupying 80,000 square feet on the top floors of a new highrise, these offices also enjoy a 360-degree view of the Atlanta skyline and, on the top floor, ceilings rising to a generous 14-foot height. Facilities provided include executive offices at the building perimeter, boardroom, break room, computer center, training center, and library. Display areas throughout supplement the racecar by showcasing other aluminum products with which the client is involved. ASD's services for Alumax involved programming, schematic design, design development, furniture selection and specification, construction documentation, construction administration, and, finally, coordination of the move-in.

Above, right: *View down stairwell to reception desk.*
Right: *Boardroom with vaulted wood ceiling*

ASD

Disney Development Company
Team Disney Offices
Lake Buena Vista, Florida

This 400,000-square-foot facility for Team Disney had to accommodate not only the usual reception and office spaces, but also an unusual number of employee amenities, such as cafeteria, dining room, fitness center with showers and locker rooms, a credit union, and a travel agency. The interiors also had to respond to an architectural shell that was dramatic and highly idiosyncratic. To integrate all these parts into a cohesive whole, ASD designed stripped-down interiors that are quiet and unobtrusive, colored primarily with a series of grays and silvers and creating a sense of light, space, and softness. With the dramatic exceptions of four-floor-high murals at the ends of the building, these sophisticated interiors are reductive, sensitive, and supportive of the surrounding architecture and the varied activities within it.

Above: An executive office.
Right: Detail of executive beverage station.
Photography: Chroma, Inc. (George Cott).

Left: *Boardroom.*
Below: *The credit union.*
Bottom of page, left: *Typical departmental reception area, looking towards atrium.*
Bottom of page, right: *Typical open plan working core.*

NationsBank
Direct Banking Center
Wichita, Kansas

A former department store was renovated to create this 70,000-square-foot office for 580 bank employees. Density is high in the facility's call center, yet the client demanded an attractive work environment and a feeling of spaciousness. The design responds to this mandate by exposing the overhead structure and mechanical services in many areas to maximize height, and by creating translucent glass walls for lounge areas and conference rooms. Workstation clusters have been arranged in diagonal patterns, allowing the stations to "borrow" space from adjacent aisles and to avoid direct face-to-face contact with neighbor-

Right, above: *Beyond a work area, a wall with circular openings.*
Right: *Breakroom.*
Below: *Second-floor reception area with workstations beyond.*
Photography: *Chroma, Inc. (George Cott)*

Right: Visitors' waiting, elevator lobby area beneath a dropped ceiling plane.
Right, below: Diagonal line of workstations.

ing stations. These open work areas are supplemented by private offices, conference and training rooms, a break room, and employee lounges. A sense of movement through the installation's two floors derives from semicircular dropped ceiling planes and from whimsically placed circular openings in walls. Steel gray carpet and panel fabrics provide a quiet, industrial backdrop for the bright accent colors that are used through-out in combinations that are never repeated. Other materials include medium-density fiber board, oriented strand board, poplar, and glass. Furnishings mix new designs and classic modern pieces from mid-century.

ASD

Moving Comfort
Chantilly, Virginia

Moving Comfort, founded in 1977, is a firm engaged in the design and international distribution of women's athletic wear. "We believe a fit woman is a powerful woman," the company's two women owners say. "And we take pride in making clothes that encourage a woman on the path to fitness and power." This facility, containing a showroom and offices for administration and distribution, was designed by ASD with that philosophy in mind. It occupies 17,000 square feet within the shell of a former warehouse that was completely gutted. The focus of the design is on product display, and the overall character is energetic, practical, and progressive. Working within a strict budget, the designers have made their effects largely with humble materials such as paint and drywall, capitalizing on the contributions of texture and vibrant color.

Ballinger

One Commerce Square

2005 Market Street

Suite 1500

Philadelphia

Pennsylvania 19103.7088

215.665.0900

215.665.0980 (Fax)

Ballinger

Johnson & Johnson
Consumer Franchises Worldwide Headquarters
Skillman, New Jersey

Right: New entrance design with glass curtain wall.
Below: Entrance lobby with reception desk and access control in foreground.
Photography: Paul Warchol.

Winner of a 1997 design excellence award from the Philadelphia chapter of the American Institute of Architects, this 450,000-square-foot facility for Johnson & Johnson is the result of thoroughly renovating a former diaper manufacturing plant, a building that was "a huge box." The box was punctured — and the vast space organized — by the insertion of a series of internal spaces flooded with natural light from new skylights. The centerpiece of these spaces is the elliptical room (seen above) flanked by the building's major conference and meeting rooms. At one end of the ellipse is the redesigned building entrance and lobby; at the other, the cafeteria for the building's 500 employees. Ballinger's services in this case included programming, space planning, architecture, engineering, and interior design.

Top of page: *Connecting "street" through the building courtyard.*
Above: *Central break-out room adjoining perimeter meeting rooms.*

Ballinger

IKON Office Solutions
Worldwide Headquarters
Malvern, Pennsylvania

Left: *Skylit atrium lobby with connecting stairs.*
Below: *Executive boardroom with on-demand video-teleconferencing.*
Photography: *Don Pearse.*

In the business of office technology and products, the client naturally wanted interiors that would reflect the latest thinking in office design. Relocation to this new three-floor, 115,000-square-foot facility marked a significant reengineering of IKON operations: from a traditional, closed office environment to an open plan encouraging internal communication. Universally-sized offices offer the maximum in flexibility. Office neighborhoods are supplemented by team rooms, centralized reproduction and networked operations, and there are also training rooms, demonstration and exhibit rooms, technology showrooms, conference rooms, a cafeteria, and a fitness center. Ballinger's design showcases the company's technology and supports interaction through openness, gen-

erous use of glass, and modular componentry. Materials are cherry wood, frosted glass, patterned carpets, and painted highlights in a palette of red (from IKON's logo), medium blue, squash yellow, and Irish green. The facility accommodates 250 employees.

Top of page: *Breakout area for customer support training center.* **Above:** *Food service area and cafeteria.*

Ballinger

Crown Cork & Seal Company, Inc.
Worldwide Headquarters
Philadelphia, Pennsylvania

Left, above: *Detail of the steel, glass, and stone stair.*
Left, below: *Lobby/waiting area. Above the suspended second-floor balcony is the boardroom suite.*
Right: *A view of the stair scissoring through the atrium.*
Photography: *Jeff Goldberg @ Esto Photographer*

Crown, an international leader in the manufacture of container packaging, is proud of its tradition of an open, interactive culture, based on a long-held belief that the exchange of ideas and information sharpens competitive advantage. An architectural expression of that view, in this new 230,000-square-foot, freestanding structure, is a three-story-high commons area. The space is penetrated by stairs and bridges connecting all levels and is open to the building's radiating office wings. In those wings, some workstations are in low-paneled office landscape systems, some are in offices with demountable glass walls. Woods employed include steamed beech veneer panels and select hard white maple, stones include Kasota from Minnesota and Burlington from England, and also prominent are aluminum and glass curtain walls and flooring of terrazzo and patterned carpet. For the building, which houses 600, Ballinger performed a full range of services: master planning, architecture, interior design, and mechanical, electrical, and plumbing engineering. The color palette, including soft gray and a muted teal, is taken from Crown's traditional company colors.

Above: Scatter-system servery for the 180-seat cafeteria.
Right: Full-height glazed office walls are demountable.

Berger Rait Design Associates, Inc.

20 Exchange Place

28th Floor

New York

New York 10005

212.742.7000

212.742.7001 (Fax)

brda@mindspring.com

www.bergerrait.com

Berger Rait Design Associates, Inc.

Murray Hill Properties
New York, New York

Right: Reception and visitor waiting area.
Below: Conference room.
Photography: Mark Ross.

Murray Hill Properties, a real estate investment firm, hired Berger Rait Design Associates to supply a full range of interiors services for the renovation of 12,000 square feet in New York. Design problems faced by Berger Rait included the accommodation of broker offices with support facilities nearby, the admission of natural light into as much of the space as possible, and the creation of a high-end image on a less-than-high-end budget. Because the real estate brokers at Murray Hill work in pairs, a standard two-person office design was developed. These offices occupy the building perimeter in this design, with interior areas devoted to conference rooms and support areas. Frosted glass panels allow the inward transmission of exterior light. Fine materials such as stone flooring and mahogany millwork make a strong first impression in the reception area, with less expensive treatments used elsewhere.

Berger Rait Design Associates, Inc.

Weekly Reader Corporation
Stamford, Connecticut

Right: General work area.
Below: Connecting corridor with conference room at left.
Photography: Mark Ross.

The design of this 30,000-square-foot facility for a publishing company represented a dramatic shift in that company's organization of its 200-person staff. The shift was from private offices clustered in separate departments (editorial, advertising, graphics, etc.) to open plan workstations clustered in project teams. The desired result:easier interaction and better communication. Supplementing the general work areas for the teams are a few private offices, a pre-press/ manufacturing center, and a large print and photography library. Services performed by Berger Rait included space planning, site selection, design development, construction documents, furniture selection, and project administration. Materials are gypsum board, fabric-covered panels, carpet tile, and — in the reception area — ceramic flooring and a striking metallic ceiling. The color palette is predominantly neutral, with bold accent colors defining the team areas.

Top of page: *Another view of a general work area.*
Above: *The reception area.*

Berger Rait Design Associates, Inc.

Barnes & Noble College Division New York, New York

The College Division of Barnes & Noble, which supervises a chain of college retail bookstores, has new quarters designed by Berger Rait in an older, landmarked New York building, and the design solution employed here manages to emphasize both old and new. A parade of existing iron columns — tall, closely spaced, and in the Composite Order — has been painted a dark, warm gray and is now an important visual (as well as structural) element of the interior. Complementing the columns is a newly inserted steel stair with wire mesh parapets. The custom-designed workstations, however, are modern as can be and have been designed in a "universal" concept for maximum flexibility. These workstations have been given prime locations along the perimeter window walls, with interior spaces devoted to private offices and support areas. The quiet, unifying color scheme is gray and white, with the addition of soft accent colors. In all, the Barnes & Noble quarters occupy 45,000 square feet spread over three floors.

Above, left:
Conference room with
library shelving.
Above: Corridor with
wall display of college
mugs.
Left: Existing columns
have become a design
feature.

Brennan Beer Gorman
Monk / Interiors

515 Madison Avenue

New York

New York 10022

212.888.7667

212.935.3868 (Fax)

1030 15th Street NW   13F Lyndhurst Tower

Suite 900   1 Lyndhurst Terrace

Washington, DC 20005   Central, Hong Kong

202.452.1644   852.2525.9766

202.452.1647 (Fax)   852.2525.9850 (Fax)

Brennan Beer Gorman Monk / Interiors

Broadcast Studio
Washington, DC

Right: Workstations beneath dropped ceiling planes.
Below: Reception and waiting area, with technical operations center at left.
Photography: Dan Cunningham.

A broadcast studio facility presented the designers with some unusual challenges: not only the expected acoustic and visual controls, but also some unseen demands such as short cable runs from operations center to studios. This last demand was satisfied by vertical stacking in the two-floor scheme that totals 58,000 square feet. The upper level holds the lobby/reception area, the main conference room, and the technology-rich operations center/master control center, this last space a striking presence in the reception area through a glass wall. The lower level, reached by a generously scaled open steel stair, holds 11 broadcasting studios, more conference areas, and over a hundred workstations. Above the workstations, floating ceiling planes improve the acoustics and add a sense of territoriality. Further challenges came with a limited budget and extremely tight time constraints, the "fast-track" project being accomplished in only 18 weeks from initial design to occupancy.

Detail, upper left:
Perforated metal panels modulate the light.
Above: *Open steel stair connecting the two*

Brennan Beer Gorman Monk / Interiors

Below: *Conference room with reception area beyond.*
Photography: *Dan Cunningham*

National Safety Council
Washington, DC

The mandate for this top-floor, 15,000-square-foot Washington office was an interior design that would foster inter-action among the 40 employees. A major step toward this goal was the minimalization of pri-vate office space and the maximization of public areas flexible enough for a variety of functions. Prominent among these areas is a central library and study area that can be divided into three smaller conference rooms. Here and throughout, changes in room configuration are accomplished by custom-designed translucent fiberglass panels sliding on tracks. Public corri-dors are unusually wide, adding to the sense of spaciousness, and some

Below, both views:

The library is divisible by
translucent panels into
three conference areas.

elements have been set
at an angle to preclude
any feeling of regimen-
tation. More fiberglass
panels obscure the
reception area's unat-
tractive view, but admit
plenty of light. Other
materials employed
include maple, stainless
steel, and plastic lami-
nates in both brushed

metal and terra-cotta
colored finishes. The
budget was a modest
$33. per square foot.

Brennan Beer Gorman Monk / Interiors

Generation Partners
New York, New York

Table lamps casting a warm glow on tabletops of American black cherry and terrazzo, simple slat-back chairs with upholstered seats, hardwood flooring — these elements generate an almost domestic warmth. Other elements in this installation — concrete ceiling slabs, exposed lozenge-shaped ducts, track lighting, low partitions, and walls of both clear and frosted glass between rooms — contribute an air of loft-like openness. Together, the elements combine to provide an environment of simplicity, quality, and comfort for the 5,200-square-foot office for a venture capital fund. A conference room seats 10-12 people, and smaller, more informal meetings are accommodated with tables and chairs along the generously scaled circulation spine that connects the reception area to the partners's offices. The budget was $287,000.

Above: Reception area.
Left: A partner's office combines loft-like simplicity with residential warmth.
Photography: Peter Paige.

55

Above and below:
Two views of the wide central corridor, alcoves furnished for casual meetings, and adjacent office areas.

Burt Hill Kosar
Rittelmann Associates

650 Smithfield Street
Suite 2600
Pittsburgh
Pennsylvania 15222.3907
412.394.7000
412.394.7880 (Fax)

400 Morgan Center
Butler
Pennsylvania 16001.5977

724.285.4761
724.285.6815 (Fax)

Mellon Bank Center
1735 Market Street
53rd Floor
Philadelphia
Pennsylvania 19103.2921
215.751.2900
215.751.2901 (Fax)

1056 Thomas Jefferson Street, NW
Washington, DC 20007
202.333.2711
202.333.3159 (Fax)

300 Brickstone Square
Andover
Massachusetts 01810
978.474.6405
978.474.6401 (Fax)

Burt Hill Kosar Rittelmann Associates

Deloitte & Touche, LLP
One PPG Place
Pittsburgh, Pennsylvania

When two giant accounting firms (Deloitte Haskins & Sells and Touche Ross) recently merged, a number of commissions materialized for combining their offices. In Pittsburgh, one of the firms had occupied a floor in PPG Place when new space on two and half adjacent floors became available. The consolidated installation, totaling 73,000 square feet, is seen here. Its three and a half floors are linked by a spiral stair with carpeted treads and parapets of curved glass. For economy, a major portion of the furniture owned by the two earlier firms was re-used, and the new interior architectural design therefore combines two distinctive styles: traditional elements in dark cherry, and more contemporary pieces in light maple. A unifying decorative device, used throughout, recalls the Union Jack. Upholstery fabrics, another unifying factor, are in deep jewel tones of burgundy, emerald, and plum, and other materials include green etched glass and brass. Since completion of the project, Burt Hill Kosar Rittelmann has been commissioned by the client for additional offices in two other cities.

Burt Hill Kosar Rittelmann Associates

Penn Avenue Place
Office Retail Complex
Pittsburgh, Pennsylvania

Penn Avenue Place is the result of an enormous undertaking: the conversion of a century-old, 650,000-square-foot former department store into a modern, highly flexible work environment. The unusually large floor areas (72,000 square feet each) were modified by converting the former bank of escalators into a new seven-floor-high atrium, ensuring that 85 percent of all workspaces are within 50 feet of natural daylight. The historic building shell has been restored and updated with new mechanical and electrical systems, new lighting, new roof, new windows, and a new "intelligent" vertical transportation system. Office spaces throughout have been given a 6-inch raised access floor. And all was accomplished on an accelerated schedule: only twelve months from vacating the old building to occupying the renovation. Two-thirds of the building is occupied by Blue Cross, 18,000 square feet on the 8th floor is occupied by a performing arts academy, its quarters also designed by Burt Hill Kosar Rittelmann, and the ground floor holds 59,000 square feet of streetfront retail space. Client Byron Falchetti of Standard Property Corporation terms the result "A super job!"

Above, right: Reception area.
Above: Atrium.
Right: Members of the Civic Light Opera, a building tenant, enjoy a break.
Opposite, above: Elevator cab interior.
Opposite, below: Paneled walkway past managers' offices.
Photography: Ed Massery.

Burt Hill Kosar Rittelmann Associates

Buchanan Ingersoll
Corporate Headquarters
Pittsburgh, Pennsylvania

The building evaluation, space planning, and design process for this 345 employee law firm led to an unusual solution: the splitting of the total 154,000 square feet into two locations in adjacent buildings. The less expensive structure with larger floor areas houses administrative offices and support space; the other houses attorney offices, managing partner's office, reception, conference and meeting rooms, and the firm's library. Attorney floors enjoy a neutral color scheme, the conference room floor a richer palette of greens and gold. Other materials are cherry paneling, marble, etched glass, and textile and vinyl wall coverings. Client satisfaction has led to commissions for five of the law firm's branch offices.

Left: Managing partner's office.
Right, above: Corridor intersection.
Right: Moses Hampton room, attorney dining named for firm's founder.
Photography: Ed Massery

Left, above: *Reception area on a floor devoted to client services that also features 16 conference and meeting rooms in a unique configuration.*

Left: *Typical secretarial workstation grouped in a cluster to promote cross-training and teamwork.*

Left, below: *Gerald W. Malky break-out room adjacent to several larger conference rooms.*

Cole Martinez Curtis and Associates

310 Washington Blvd.

Suite 116

Marina del Rey

California 90292

310.827.7200

310.822.5803 (Fax)

Cole Martinez Curtis and Associates

National Telephone & Communications
Irvine, California

The two design goals seemed, at first, to be contrary to one another. The first was to provide a high-tech facility for National Telephone & Communications, Inc. (NTC), a long-distance telephone company that employs multi-level marketing techniques. The company's new 75,000-square-foot headquarters needed to reflect its commitment to competing on the highest level in the telecommunications industry. The company's multi-level marketing, however, involves family and friends, and the second goal was to reflect a warm, friendly environment reflecting family ties and values. Both goals seem satisfied in this solution. The campus-like, single-story facility is in three units, which enclose a large open-air courtyard. The units and all their busily working components are linked by an eight-foot-wide "tour corridor." Here groups of prospective representatives are taken on tours, viewing work in progress through large expanses

Left, top of page:
Exterior monument sign
with client logo.
Left, center:
Main reception area
overlooking open-air
courtyard.
Left, bottom of page:
"Tour corridor" through-
out the facility allows
viewing of all depart-
ments in action.
Photography: Toshi
Yoshimi

**Right, above and
below:** Two views of the
reception and visitor
waiting area for the U.S.
Leadership Group.

of bronze-tinted glass. Entrances to departments have been developed into marble-floored alcoves where tour guides can pause and explain the work being done, and adjacent kiosks of wood and stainless steel hold exhibitions with further explanations. Each tour ends in the open patio, where catered lunches are served. The cost of the NTC facility averages $70. a square foot. A happy outcome of the design process and its result: NTC is so pleased with the design that it has hired Cole Martinez Curtis and Associates to design other business centers throughout the United States, Europe, and the Pacific Rim.

Right, above: *A private executive office of the U.S. Leadership Group.*
Right below: *A conference room for the same group.*

Cole Martinez Curtis and Associates

Countrywide Home Loans, Inc. Corporate Headquarters Calabasas, California

Formerly a Lockheed Corporation facility, this 205,000-square-foot building on four levels wraps around a light-filled open-air atrium. Cole Martinez Curtis and Associates has transformed the building into a new headquarters for Countrywide Home Loans, a fast-growing organization that is the nation's largest independent mortgage lender. Attached to the main building by a covered walkway is a separate conference center with an additional 20,000 square feet. Within the main building, the 35,000-square-foot top floor, enjoying 11- and 12-foot ceiling heights, is dedicated to executive use, its generously scaled reception area open to the main building entrance and lobby below. Top-floor offices have been reduced from a depth of 30 feet to 21 feet, thus creating a wide executive secretarial corridor outside the offices, a space that doubles as a gallery for the client's extensive art collection. On floors below, 85 percent of the employees are accommodated in open-plan workstations, 15 percent in private offices. Throughout, a California atmosphere is created with a color palette of light greens and tans, accented with carpets of darker green and doors and millwork of

Below: Left, above: Conference room in an executive office suite. **Left:** *Another part of an executive office suite.* **Photography:** *Toshi Yoshimi.*

70

American walnut. Cole Martinez Curtis and Associates performed a full scope of interior design services, including space planning and graphic design. The reported costs averaged $31.50 per square foot.

Above: *On the third floor, the executive reception area overlooks the atrium.*
Right: *The executive secretarial corridor.*

71

Top of page: The boardroom.
Above, left: The legal department and its large skylight.
Above, right: A group of open plan workstations.

Diversified
Interior Design Inc.

2120 Arch Street

Philadelphia

Pennsylvania 19103-1308

215.567.3132

215.568.2639 (Fax)

Diversified Interior Design Inc. Penn Mutual Life Insurance Company Headquarters Renovations Philadelphia, Pennsylvania

Penn Mutual's headquarters building in Philadelphia is a 17-story, 28-year-old building that had come to require functional and aesthetic upgrades in all of its public spaces in order to meet both code requirements and modern expectations. New amenities included computerized elevator cabs, a concierge desk, and new furnishings. The lobby's new materials palette of granite, glass, and metal finishes was designed to enhance the client's important N.C. Wyeth painting depicting William Penn's treaty with the Indians. Public areas on tenant floors were also redesigned, as were an extended street level entrance and a top-floor boardroom, used for both audiovisual presentations and luncheons. Energy efficiency was addressed by means of a new lighting concept. In all, the renovations covered 350,000 square feet.

Left: *Entrance lobby with N.C. Wyeth painting.*
Photography:
Don Pearse.

Above Right:
*Renovated and expand-
ed building entrance.*
Above: *View of new
elevator cabs and tenant
lobbies.*
Right: *17th-floor
boardroom.*

Diversified Interior Design Inc.

Crozer Keystone Health System
Springfield Hospital - Healthplex
Springfield, Pennsylvania

The Crozer Keystone Health System bought the Springfield Hospital, a 100-bed community facility, with a plan to remodel and extensively expand it in accordance with a community needs assessment and survey. The scope of work included 100,000 square feet of renovation and 186,000 square feet new construction. The result, the Crozer Keystone Healthplex, now offers a continuum of services including surgery, rehab, and wellness programs. Medical practice suites, emergency and intensive care units were upgraded, and new construction accommodates four new operating rooms, an endoscopy suite, a special procedures unit, an outpatient radiology center, a women's imaging center, a cardiology and pulmonary wellness unit, a decontamination/sterile unit, a medical office building, a health club, and more. All these components are linked by a new "mall" of circulation spaces and adjoining, intimately scaled waiting areas.

Opposite, above: Color and pattern brighten an ICU area. **Opposite, below:** Waiting area seen from corridor. **Left:** Typical waiting area. **Below, left:** One of the outpatient clinical areas. **Below, right:** Terrazzo-floored lobby link between Health Mall and existing hospital. **Photography:** Don Pearse. **Architectural Consultant:** Francis Cauffman Foley Hoffmann, Architects Ltd.

Diversified Interior Design Inc.

Penn State Geisinger Health System Corporate Headquarters Consolidation Harrisburg, Pennsylvania

The Penn State Geisinger Health System brought together two major health care providers in Central Pennsylvania. This required that the leadership of both systems move to a central location so that daily management and planning of future ventures could be accomplished efficiently and creatively. This 17,000 SF central location also allowed for easy access for regional administrators to come together for training, and periodic meetings.

Along with these priorities, Diversified Interior Design was commissioned to create a new integrated image for two established systems, design for state-of-the-art communication technology, and accomplish all these tasks in six months. The "V" shaped floor plan of the chosen building gave Diversified Interior Design the opportunity to create zones of space that answered the issue of public vs. private by grouping the meeting spaces around the lobby at the intersection of the two wings, create a private suite for the four chief executives and their support staff in one wing and plan for executive staff in the opposite wing.

Image considerations and the need for the newly formed system to communicate its stability and forward thinking were answered by establishing a classic contemporary theme to all spaces and materials such as cherry, etched glass, fabric accents were utilized to communicate the warmth of a company focused on health care. A neutral palette of colors gives the space a timeless quality and allowed for

an art work collection that communicates home and hearth including Pennsylvania artists in all media from contemporary quilts, to lithographic reproductions by Andrew Wyeth.

Above, left: *The receptionist location allowing for proper scheduling of the boardroom and training center while receiving daily guests.*
Above, right: *Administrative assistants are clustered in a team environment for maximum support of the health system leadership.*
Right: *Reception area and waiting doubles as a break-out lounge for boardroom and training center.*
Far right: *The Boardroom utilized flexible lighting and a demountable table system to allow for teleconferencing and videoconferencing along with large formal meetings.*
Photography: *Don Pearse.*

Diversified Interior Design Inc.

Bristol-Myers Squibb Shared Services Princeton, New Jersey

Below: View of team modules.
Bottom, left: The director's office.
Bottom, right: Team conference rooms.

Photography: Don Pearse.
Architectural consultant: Francis Cauffman Foley Hoffmann, Architects Ltd.

Using "fast-track" methodology, Diversified Interior Design worked with Bristol-Myers Squibb Company Real Estate and Facilities Management Group on this 160,000-square-foot office space. It houses 600 employees whose work supports the company's in-house operations. A primary goal of the project was to create a facility that would encourage informal communication and foster a team approach to project management. The design firm's services included master planning, programming, building evaluation, full-service fit-out of the interiors, and move management. A critical element was the selection of a furniture system manufacturer based on an analysis of several systems' ability to enhance work flow.

DMJM Rottet

3250 Wilshire Boulevard

Los Angeles

California 90010.1599

213.368.2888

213.381.2773 (Fax)

DMJM Rottet

This 40,000-square-foot law firm has won not only an Honor Award for Interior Architecture from the California Council of the American Institute of Architects, but also a "Best Law Office" award from the American Bar Association. Although the venerable firm of McCutchen, Doyle, Brown & Enersen has a history dating back to 1883, it now has an average partner age of only 45 and is at the forefront of current issues such as healthcare and the environmental law. The design of its quarters, therefore, needed to be energetic and progressive, while still satisfying the firm's wide range of clients, including major corporations and nonprofit groups. The reception area is distinguished by two focal walls, one pyramidal in form, the other a panel of art glass commissioned from artist Linda Hudson, this last transmitting light while giving privacy to an adjacent conversation area. The spatial organization, offices, and circulation areas are traditional, but with an emphasis on exposure to natural light, and key materials are natural woods and a variety of custom glass selections.

McCutchen, Doyle, Brown & Enersen
Law Offices
Los Angeles, California

Above, right: Detail of the glass art wall.
Below left: Glass wall and pyramid wall in reception area.
Photography: Nick Merrick, Hedrich-Blessing.

Below, right: Interconnecting stair.
Bottom of page: Open office area.
Opposite: Entry view of reception area.

DMJM Rottet

Investment Management Firm Corporate Headquarters Los Angeles, California

Having occupied four contiguous floors of a Los Angeles tower for 17 years, this globally prominent financial consulting and investments firm eagerly grabbed the opportunity to expand into two additional levels. It decided on renovation of its existing space as well, and even leased the building's 55th-floor "penthouse" topping the whole package. This highest level, formerly used for storage, had a distinct advantage — a 40-foot ceiling height — but also a distinct flaw — no windows. In this unusual space DMJM Rottet have designed a dining facility, pre-function room, conference rooms, and a 100-seat auditorium where weekly presentations are made, the lack of outside light being deemed ideal for lighting control in this last element. A partial mezzanine was also inserted for further expansion. Down below, the company's egalitarian policies prevail, with newcomers and senior executives being assigned identical offices, with prime corner locations going to rooms for group assembly rather than private spaces, and with even conference tables being round or elliptical, not rectangular. Cove lighting and sculptural light baffles add overhead interest, makore is the principal wood for millwork and custom cabinetry.

Left: A typical private office.
Right, top of page: The "penthouse" reception area.
Right, middle: Dining area.
Right: New stairway linking seven levels.
Opposite page: The 53rd floor reception area.
Photography: Nick Merrick, Hedrich-Blessing.

DMJM Rottet

The Walt Disney Company
Feature Animation Northside Offices
Burbank, California

DMJM Rottet's complete renovation of this Disney facility for computer-based animation artists encompasses four floors of work space and an adjacent commissary and function rooms, all totaling 225,000 square feet. Included are a computer graphics facility, editing and viewing rooms, production suites, a game room, a snack bar, a fitness room, an employee store, and private offices and open office pods. These last are assigned by "alternative officing" techniques and are easily modified, thus attaining maximum flexibility. The office and production spaces are the first of their kind for this company, accommodating completely new and still-evolving computer technology. The DMJM Rottet design team has given particular attention to issues of lighting regulation and power cabelling, insuring future functionality.

Top of page: Corridor and work area.
Above: Digital review room.
Right: Commissary.
Photography: Nick merrick, Hedrich-Blessing.

86

Left: *Second floor elevator lobby and pre-function area.*
Below: *Two views looking from reception area towards entry.*

DMJM Rottet

Pontiac Land Private Ltd. Executive Headquarters Singapore

Pontiac Land Private Ltd. is one of Singapore's pre-eminent real estate deveopment companies. It selected DMJM Rottet to design suitably impressive quarters on the 17,000-square-foot penthouse level of architect Kevin Roche's 41-floor tower. Window views across Singapore are spectacular, but views inside the offices themselves offer ample delights of their own. The interior design reflects both Occidental and Oriental precedents and incorporates a world-class selection of art, furnishings, and materials. Traditional screens are reinterpreted, for example, in gridded mahogany panels, and custom conference tables have tops and bases of white marble. During the nine-month design process, the DMJM team made three trips to Singapore, the clients three to California, with additional presentations made via video cassettes based on computer renderings and a scale model.

Below: White fabric-covered ceiling and wood screens in the office of Pontiac Land partner Liong Seen. **Photography:** Nick Merrick, Hedrich-Blessing

Ellerbe Becket

800 LaSalle Avenue
Minneapolis
Minnesota 55402
612.376.2000
612.376.2271 (Fax)

Kansas City
Washington, DC
San Francisco
Phoenix
Los Angeles

Moscow
Wakefield
Seoul
Tokyo

Ellerbe Becket

Lommen, Nelson, Cole & Stageberg, PA
Minneapolis, Minnesota

Two tenant floors totalling 30,000 square feet in a downtown Minneapolis high-rise is the locale. Two recently merged law firms constituted the client. A modest $25. per square foot was the budget. From initial programming through construction documents to selection of art, plants and accessories was the scope of work. An impression of tradition, establishment, and quality was the desired — and achieved — effect. "Up front" spaces, visited by clients and guests, include a generous reception area, an adjoining conference center, and, at the top of the open stairs, a law library. These areas were finished with silk wallcoverings, painted paneling, and floors of Brazilian cherry. Other areas, including the accounting department, lunchroom, and offices and workstations for a staff of 100, have vinyl wallcovering and carpet. The total result earned a first place award in the regional design competition of the American Society of Interior Designers.

Far right: The law library on the upper floor.
Other three views: The cherry-floored reception area and, beyond the glass-paned doors, elements of the conference center.
Photography: Jon Miller @ Hedrich-Blessing.

Ellerbe Becket

Deloitte & Touche
Wilton, Connecticut

Above: A row of glass-enclosed 'phone booths in an executive area corridor.
Left: Glass-topped desk in the reception area.
Below: Detail of indirect pendant lighting, with a reflection of daylight from the long skylight.
Photography: Chuck Choi, NIC, Ltd.

Below: In the exective
area, curved metal parti-
tions are suspended
from the ceiling.
Bottom of page: A
detail of the reception
desk construction.

This Connecticut installation, winner of a nation-
al Interiors Award of
Excellence from the
American Institute of
Architects, houses offices
for one of the country's
leading accounting
firms. Its total area is
110,000 square feet,
with a tenth of that
space devoted to the
executive areas shown
here. Other spaces
include a television stu-
dio, training facilities,
and management and
clerical areas. The con-
text is a Kevin Roche/
John Dinkeloo building
designed in the '60s, and
the interiors capitalize
on building features
such as the skylight run-
ning the length of the
space. Newly inserted
elements of stone,
wood, metal, and glass
are disposed in an
abstract composition in
which parts slide past
one another to create an
effect of spatial continu-
ity. Ellerbe Becket's services in this case included programming, plan-
ning, design, construc-
tion documents, con-
struction administration,
and the design and spec-
ification of furniture and
signage.

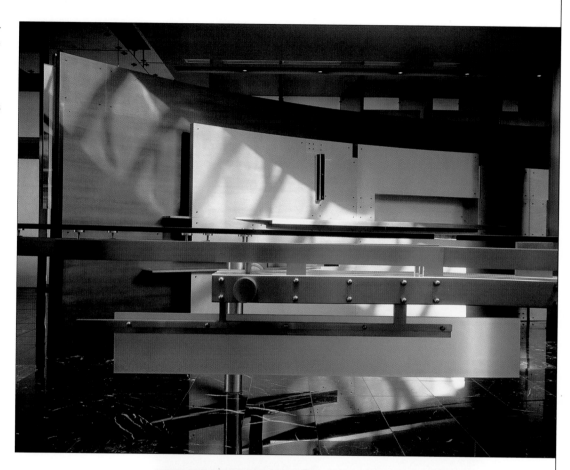

Ellerbe Becket

Ecolab Inc.
Corporate Headquarters
St. Paul, Minnesota

Right: The boardroom.
Below: A spare grouping of comfortable seating in the reception area.
Photography: Koyama Photographic.

Ecolab is a corporation engaged in developing premium cleaning, sanitizing, and maintenance products for the hospitality, institutional, and industrial markets. Employing more than 9,500, it operates in 34 countries. This 8,000-square-foot executive suite, completed in 1997, is on the 19th floor of its downtown St. Paul headquarters building and houses the offices of Ecolab's President/CEO and Chairman, administrative support areas, boardroom, conference room, video conference room, kitchen, and reception area. The requisite image of a successful, dynamic, and forward-thinking company registers in the first impression of a generously scaled and minimally furnished reception room. From here, light is transmitted, through a custom-designed curving wall of cast glass, into the adjacent boardroom, which seats two dozen.

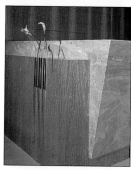

Top of page: *Curved glass wall in the conference room.*
Above, left: *Reception area seating with reception desk beyond.*
Above, right: *Lounge seating area in an executive office.*
Left: *Detail of the reception desk.*

Ellerbe Becket

Riverside Bank
Minneapolis, Minnesota

Ellerbe Becket's charge was the development of a 4,900-square-foot downtown branch of a small community bank. The bank's existing reputation for friendliness and accessibility needed to be expressed, and problems of an awkwardly proportioned plan and limited public visibility needed to be overcome. The solution angles a teller line toward the main entry for maximum exposure and modulates space with ceiling heights that vary from nine to eleven feet. Tilted wall planes, used throughout, add interest and vitality, and generous use of clear and frosted glass give a greater sense of openness than conventional partitions would have allowed. The color scheme contrasts light and dark neutrals, and furnishings are kept simple and small-scaled. At $54. a square foot, the cost was $265,000.

Left, top: Retail banking teller line.
Left, middle: Circular information/reception desk.
Left, bottom: Workstations surrounding the desk are for loan officers and bankers.
Photography: Terry Wilkenson.

The Environments Group

303 East Wacker Drive

Suite 800

Chicago

Illinois 60601

312.644.5080

312.644.5299 (Fax)

The Environments Group

Andersen Consulting Technology Park
Northbrook, Illinois

Below: Visitors' lobby and waiting area.
Photography: Steve Hall, Hedrich-Blessing.

The installation seen here involved the relocation of 1,500 Andersen Consulting employees from downtown Chicago to the suburb of Northbrook and the renovation of 320,000 square feet of existing office space to accommodate them. Serving as a working laboratory for Andersen's latest concept of the ideal working environment, the alternative office configurations used employ the maximum in both spatial and technological flexibility. Included are semi-private enclosed workspaces and workstations, "hotelling" or "just in time" workstations for more mobile workers, and a variety of teaming spaces for informal groups of six to eight. Because the space is on four floors that are large (80,000 square feet each) and awkwardly shaped, the design incorporates breakout areas with brightly colored curvilinear feature walls, serving as wayfinding elements at the junctions of building wings. Also provided were a cafeteria, conference center, data center, fitness center, and a series of client presentation spaces. Despite its size, the project was accomplished in 12 months, and with a high degree of client satisfaction. According to Ronald L. Cullum, Andersen's office managing partner, the design firm "truly understands how to collect design program information; they got to know our people and requirements very well. The employees and partners of our firm view The Environments Group's design solutions throughout the building as unique and innovative, highly responsive to a variety of user needs, and yet also very cost effective: an excellent investment."

Above: *Open offices with teaming area.*
Left: *Cafeteria servery.*

The Environments Group

The Florsheim Group
Chicago, Illinois

This 125,000-square-foot headquarters for a century-old footwear manufacturer and retailer reflects Florsheim's product in many ways. Relocating here from previous quarters that were basically unchanged since the '30s gave both clients and designers the opportunity to study and resolve issues of work process and workplace image. Working closely with Florsheim's chairman, Charles J. Campbell, and meeting with shoemakers in order to understand the fabrication process, the design team established key areas for identity expression. For these, forms and materials were chosen to create an extension of Florsheim's retail presence. Components of shoemaking materials (leather, needles, and thread) and process (drawings, prototypes, and finished products) are incorporated in the design in unexpected ways: shoe prototypes are etched and carved in glass, shoe leather is used on ceiling panels,

sole patterns are screened onto wall surfaces, large-scale needles become lighting fixtures, and both footprints and thread are represented in the custom carpet designs. The result is a contemporary and highly functional facility for 500 employees that respects and reflects the client's strong heritage and sense of craft. The total scope of work by The Environments Group included programming, design, construction documentation, supervision of the bidding process, and observation of construction.

Farrington
Design Group

230 Peachtree Street

Suite 2000

Atlanta

Georgia 30303.1515

404.836.3000

404.836.3100 (Fax)

www.farington.com

Farrington Design Group

Pacesetter Steel Service, Inc.
World Headquarters
Kennesaw, Georgia

Left: Conference room with custom-designed table.
Photography: Scott McDonald © Hedrich-Blessing.

Above: Workstations with views of the wooded site.
Above, right: The steel cable-suspended stair.

This 54,000-square-foot building houses the administrative center for Pacesetter Steel Service and, with many elements of its steel structure exposed, is a showcase for steel products and the steel distribution industry. It sits on a beautifully wooded 26-acre site in Kennesaw, Georgia, just north of Atlanta. After Farrington Design Group was commissioned to create the building, and after numerous meetings with the client, the designers were also asked to provide interior architectural design, furniture and fixture selection, and a corporate identity package comprising both environmental and print graphic design. The lowest of the building's three levels houses the corporate training center with seating capacity of 200, an employee cafeteria, and space set aside for a future auditorium. The middle level is occupied largely by workstations, executed in maple and organized in team groupings. On the upper level is the semi-circular marketing conference room, seating 30. Connecting all three levels is a custom-designed stair suspended from steel cables. The entire project, from design kick-off through completion of construction, was accomplished in only fourteen months.

Farrington Design Group

Premiere Technologies, Inc.
Operations Center
Atlanta, Georgia

Premiere Technologies is an Atlanta-based telecommunications and software development company. It was founded to develop a new generation of telephony-based products, networks, and services. Farrington Design Group was chosen to design the company's 24-hour technical operations center, which serves as a base for its information services and also as a showcase for its systems equipment. Beyond the ramped entrance (which satisfies ADA requirements and provides an elevated floor level for handling additional power needs) is a central foyer with audio-visual equipment on one side and computer equipment on the other. The space is subtly lighted through the perforations of a metal screen ceiling. Beyond two pairs of touch-controlled glass doors is the conference room. Here the main feature is a custom-designed table of bleached white maple, designed to conceal all electrical cabling through its center pedestal.

Left: Graduated ramps from entrance to central foyer.
Below: Central foyer with large and small monitors. Beyond a glass wall is the conference room.
Photography: ©Rion Rizzo/Creative Sources/ Atlanta.

Farrington Design Group

New York Life Insurance Company
Atlanta, Georgia

New York Life asked Farrington Design Group to design its new 30,000-square-foot regional service center in a manner reflecting the corporate values of integrity, teamwork, innovation, fun, and a sense of urgency. Facilities were to include a reception area, conference rooms, and a training room with self-contained workstations. Cherry is the primary wood used for millwork throughout the installation, accented with diamond-shaped inlays in other woods. The custom conference table repeats the diamond motif, and the conference room is separated from the reception/visitor waiting area by doors with frosted glass panels. Did the designers satisfy their client's goals? As Francis Donnelly, New York Life's Corporate Vice-President, puts it, "Farrington Design Group felt the pulse of our production-oriented organization and created a timeless, open, and efficient environment that adds value to our culture."

Farrington Design Group

Kilpatrick Stockton LLP
Atlanta, Georgia

Right: One of the conference rooms.
Below: Part of the extensive law library.
Right: Oval-shaped elevator lobby.
Photography: Jon Miller, © Hedrich-Blessing.

Kilpatrick Stockton LLP (formerly Kilpatrick & Cody) is one of Atlanta's most prestigious law firms. Its headquarters, occupies a total of 142,000 square feet on seven contiguous floors, expresses both traditional values and a progressive approach to the practice of law. The unobtrusive accommodation of technology and efficient, flexible planning were other desiderata. Farrington Design Group satisfied the need for flexibility with the development of a "universal" floor plan for the various practice groups on five of the floors, and by linking all seven levels with a monumental bronze-railed stairway. Throughout, clean detailing is expressed in figured makore and

other fine woods and in a broad palette of decorative marbles and granites. Conference tables, credenzas, and pendant lighting fixtures are among the many custom-designed components of the design. According to M. Andrew Kauss, a partner in Kilpatrick Stockton LLP, "Our offices are efficient and finished in a manner which conveys the timeless elegance we desired. Farrington succeeded in meeting our goals in all respects."

Gary Lee & Partners

1743 Merchandise Mart

Chicago

Illinois 60654

312.644.1744

312.644.1745 (Fax)

glpartners@aol.com

www.glpartners.com

Gary Lee & Partners

Gary Lee & Partners

Clune Construction Company Headquarters Chicago, Illinois

As the new owner of his own firm, Mike Clune wanted his new offices to be functional, adaptable and to represent his firm's stellar reputation in the general contracting and construction field.

Firm identity is established directly from the elevator lobby. A feature wall of construction materials (i.e., Fiberglass, plywood, exposed metal fasteners) serves as the signature element as well as the demising wall for conference rooms and private offices. Constantly changing team groups and large workspace requirements resulted in mobile workstations assembled along a technology spine supplying power and communications.

The total area of the project is 11,000 s.f.

Gary Lee & Partners

National Processing Company
Corporate Headquarters
Louisville, Kentucky

As consultants in the fast paced field of transaction technology, NPC wanted their new offices to reflect professionalism integrated with their unique technologies while featuring the marketing of their various services to their clients.

Gary Lee & Partners, in collaboration with an image consultant, designed NPC's 20,000 s.f. offices to house their seven different business units and to reflect each unit's product services in display kiosks located throughout the space. A key feature is a state of the art multi-media facility where presentations are tailored to the specific needs and interests of their clients.

Finishes were clear, reflective and in some cases transparent to support their concept.

Opposite, above:
Reception area.
Opposite, below:
Anteroom outside
multimedia room.
Above: View towards
entrance to multimedia
room.
Photography: Steve
Hall © Hedrich-Blessing.

Gary Lee & Partners

Baker & Daniels
Law Offices
Ft. Wayne, Indiana

Below: *Secretarial workstations.*
Photography: *Scott McDonald © Hedrich-Blessing.*

Below, left: *Main reception area.*
Below, right: *Stairway between floors.*

The design of Baker & Daniels new 60,000 s.f. offices in Ft. Wayne, Indiana was to reflect the success and professionalism of the law firm as well as support their functional and technological requirements.

Much of the aesthetics focused on the utilization of natural light as demonstrated through use of a predominantly light color palette, transparent feature stair and exterior corridors along the east and west ends of the floorplate. Use of stainless steel, bronze and mahogany veneers provide reflective yet contrasting accents.

Below, left: *Corridor between window wall and main conference room.*
Below, right: *Main conference room designed by Gary Lee & Partners.*

Gensler

Atlanta

Boston

Chicago

Dallas

Denver

Detroit

Hong Kong

Houston

London

Los Angeles

New York

600 California Street

Newport Beach

San Francisco

Parsippany, NJ

California 94108

San Francisco

415.433.3700

Tokyo

415.627.3737 (Fax)

Washington, DC

Gensler

**Sprint PCS
Headquarters
Irvine, California**

Right: Control console for computer technicians.
Below: Typical 140-sq.-ft. office, convertible to a conference room. Maple cabinetry is movable.
Photography: Erhard Pfeiffer.

Above: 3,000-sq.-ft. Computer room with raised floor for power supply.
Left, below: Reception area with panels of golden maple veneer, product displays, and banquette seating.

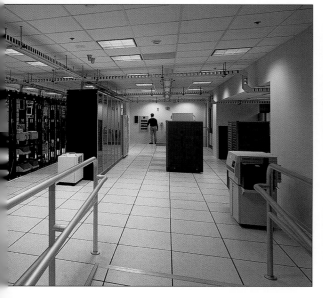

Cox Communications PCS, L.P. (doing business as Sprint PCS) is a start-up company providing personal communication services using cable network technology. When it approached Gensler, it was facing explosive growth, needing to expand its staff from four employees to 500. The fast-track project called for 110,000 square feet, comprising corporate and engineering offices on five floors, and a community service center and technology center on another. A further complication was that the 133 employees of the engineering department had to be moved into temporary space within three weeks of the request. To accomplish these goals, Gensler devised an unusual project delivery process of five construction document packages, allowing construction of some parts to begin while others were still being drawn. Similarly, the general contractor and furniture dealer were brought on board unusually early to assist in building evaluations and pre-lease services. Without an existing facility, Sprint PCS depended on Gensler's own expertise for determining furniture standards and workplace processes. Having accomplished a successful move-in in 1996, the client/designer relationship continues: Gensler has already added two more floors to the headquarters, and has also designed sales and service centers, engineering and warehouse facilities, and training centers in half a dozen locations. In addition, Gensler has been hired to design, construct, and install a customized resource management system to handle the anticipated future churn of Sprint PCS's space and personnel.

Above: *Customer care center. Groups of ten customer reps sit in clusters of serpentine workstations.*

123

Gensler

Network Equipment Technologies
Ashburn, Virginia

N.E.T., a progressive California-based supplier of multiservice networks and "backbones" for communications systems, required a regional facility near Dulles International Airport. A light industrial building shell in suburban Virginia offered low rents, high ceilings, and convenience for fly-in customers. The one-floor, 45,600-square-foot facility designed by Gensler houses a total of 155 workers in a technical support group, a product assembly group, and a customer training group. There are also laboratories, some light manufacturing, and a data/operations center. Challenges included a fast-track schedule (five months), a low budget, and high end-user expectations. In addition, there were unusual technical demands for adding infrastructure to the building that would support highly sophisticated equipment. Industrial areas needed high levels of illumination, but much of the lighting had to be glare-free. There was also a need for a design that would provide visitors with orientation and psychological release after days of intense classroom training. The budget-conscious solution employs simple forms, large planes of bold color, and large-scale graphic patterns, all executed with standard products and materials. The installation was honored with an award from the International Interior Design Association.

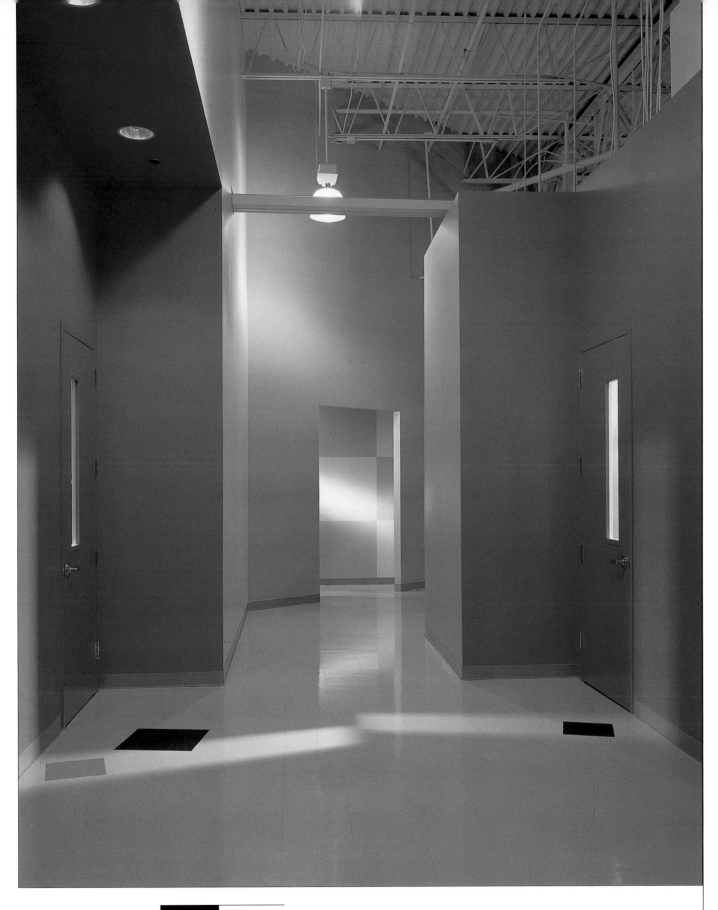

Above: *Bright colors and inset floor tiles enliven a corridor between classrooms.*

Gensler

Netscape Communications Corporation
Mountain View, California,
and
Sunnyvale, California

Right: The Netscape
General Store in
Mountain View.

On its internet site, Netscape describes itself as "A Cool Place to Work." For its own headquarters, it wanted no less. Founded in 1994, the company provides software for information exchange in a rapidly expanding market, and its own facilities are expanding similarly. Gensler's ongoing design work for Netscape consists so far of approximately 800,000 square feet in 16 buildings, and is still growing. All phases of the work have been fast-track and with a budget heavily weighted towards technology, and all have been subject to the client's need for a workplace environment that will attract and help retain a skilled, talented, and highly creative workforce. Gensler has helped Netscape address the issues of open office plans versus private offices in their efforts to minimize workplace hierarchies and establish an egalitarian, team-oriented work culture. One of the client's goals, to speed up product cycles, was achieved through creation of numerous work areas. The innovative solutions provide many small, generic, individual spaces, but also a number of vibrant, colorful, shared spaces where work teams can gather or individual workers can enjoy a quiet break. The design goal, obviously achieved, was to avoid the customary boundaries that divide work, decompression, and relaxation. Cool.

127

Above, left and right:
Two of the break areas
that provide relaxation
after long hours of
work. The area shown at
left has a checkerboard
of velcro. The other has
a pillow-strewn ban-
quette.
Right: A receptionist's
desk and visitors' wait-
ing area.

Godwin Associates

7000 Central Parkway

Suite 1020

Atlanta

Georgia 30328

770.804.1280

770.804.1284 (Fax)

Godwin Associates

iXL
Corporate Headquarters
Atlanta, Georgia

Right: One of the video edit suites.
Below: Main lobby with interactive computer modules.
Photography: Brian Robbins.

Right: *One of the team work areas.*
Below: *High-tech marketing presentation center.*

In the words of Bert Ellis, Chairman and CEO of this high-tech interactive communications company, "We wanted an office that conveyed energy, conveyed youth, and conveyed innovation." The result is Godwin Associates' design for the 30,000-square-foot corporate headquarters shown here. It occupies two and a half floors in a low-rise Atlanta office building. Facilities for iXL's 120 employees include private offices, team areas, video edit suites, a video library, conference rooms, lunch rooms, and a computer presentation marketing center. Throughout, there were exceptional requirements to be met in cabling and other communication needs. Some of this is deliberately exposed in ceiling ladder racks and in glass-walled multiple server rooms, and the expression of technology reaches a climax in the main presentation room. Other prominent design elements include multi-height colored wall panels with perforated metal shelving, surfaces of painted millwork and brushed stainless steel, acoustical ceiling treatments, and indirect lighting. The color scheme is sparked by bold primaries.

Godwin Associates

Sales Technologies Corporate Headquarters and Customer Service Center
Atlanta, Georgia

Right: Beyond the receptionist's desk, an illuminated niche displays artwork.
Below: Elevator lobby features granite, slate, metals, and bird's-eye maple.
Photography: Brian Robbins.

Sales Technologies is an Atlanta-based provider of computer hardware, software, and customer support for the health-care industry. For its operations and its 500 employees, Godwin Associates has designed two facilities totalling 130,000 square feet. Approximately half the area is on three floors of a Buckhead mid-rise office building and con-stitutes the company's corporate headquarters. Here a polished image prevails, expressed in a soft color palette of green and dusty blue and in surfaces of cherry and bird's-eye maple, granite and slate, and panels of glass with rice paper inserts.

Workstations are orga-nized by teams in areas defined by arched ceiling soffits. The other facility, in suburban Norcross, Georgia, is a one-story service center building for Sales Technologies' customer service group. It boasts 28-foot-high ceilings lit from below, loading docks for ship-ping 500 to 600 laptops per day, exposed cabling in a trapeze system, and a fleet of custom-designed stainless steel carts for the loading and testing of computer software.

Top of page: *Visitors' waiting area enjoys a view of Peachtree Street and downtown Atlanta.*
Above: *Open plan workstations, grouped in teams.*

Godwin Associates

Imlay Investments Incorporated
Atlanta, Georgia

Right: Conference room with cherry woodwork and leather seating.
Below: Comfortable seating in the CEO's private office.
Photography: Gary Knight

John Imlay, a long-term client of Godwin Associates, is the retired CEO of MSA/Dun & Bradstreet Software, a part owner of the Atlanta Falcons football franchise, and an investor in developing computer companies. His offices in a mid-rise Atlanta office building are designed to be comfortable and inviting for a variety of tasks and meetings. They include reception areas, conference facilities, work areas, an entertainment suite, and a private dining room that displays Imlay's collection of Norman Rockwell prints and originals. The color palette is gray, burgundy, teal, gold, and mauve. Responsibilities of Godwin Associates in this case included programming, space plan-

ning, interior design services from construction documentation to administration, the selection of finishes, furniture, and art, and the design of custom furniture and carpeting. The client's personal taste, however, is reflected throughout, as is a congenial clublike atmosphere.

Above, right: *Private dining area.*
Right: *The reception area establishes the motif of repeated wood blocks that is continued throughout the offices.*

Godwin Associates

**Hewlett Packard
Graphics Lab
Chapel Hill, North Carolina**

For the development of software and hardware for three-dimensional computer graphics, Godwin Associates designed this 14,000-square-foot facility in North Carolina. Around the single floor's central core are a computer laboratory, software porting lab, server room, library, shower room, and other support facilities. Prime space at the building perimeter is thus available for workstations and a series of conference rooms. The main customer conference room opening off the reception area, however, is an internal space. To provide the room with light, yet give some privacy to meeting attendees, a decorative pattern has been etched into a series of glass doors. Etched glass is used elsewhere as well, as is brushed stainless steel and custom cherry cabinetry with ebonized inlaid detailing. There is a program of limited-edition fine art prints, and the focal colors throughout are gray, gold, and an intense purple.

Above, left: Etched glass gives both privacy and light to the main conference room.
Above, right: The lobby.
Left: Conference room.
Photography: Brian Robbins.

136

Greenwell Goetz Architects, PC

1310 G Street NW

Washington D.C. 20005

202.682.0700

202.682.0738 (Fax)

Greenwell Goetz Architects, PC

Investment Company Institute
Washington, DC

The design goal, a facility advanced in its technology yet quiet in demeanor. The client, an association representing the country's financial giants. These offices needed to satisfy a diverse group of employees and committee members while projecting a favorable image for the mutual fund industry. The space of approximately 60,000 square feet contains general offices and specialized areas such as reception, boardroom with adjacent anteroom, committee rooms, staff lounge, library, support areas, and a computer room. Workstations have been customized to accommodate future as well as current technology. Natural light is brought inside providing a play of light and shadow. The light is shared with interior spaces by means of clerestories, frosted glass and clear glass. Furnishings and accessories offer some historical references for an interior that also caters to the technical demands of diverse individuals and functions.

Opposite, top:
Customized administrative workstations.
Opposite, below left:
Main reception area.
Opposite, below right:
Communicating stairway.
Above: Anteroom of a committee room.
Right: The national committee room with integrated technology.
Photography: David Patterson.

Greenwell Goetz Architects, PC

American Personal Communications/ Sprint Spectrum
Bethesda, Maryland

Spanning five levels and totaling 92,000 square feet, this headquarters installation for APC/Sprint Spectrum was developed within a tight budget and an even tighter schedule. In providing a corporate image for the new digital communications company that merged APC and Sprint, an integrated team approach of architect, contractor, and furniture dealer was instituted to achieve the design objectives in the allotted time. During the six-month project, each phase of the complete interior architectural services lasted only 60 days. The goal was to create an environment that would support the company's move to a flatter organization with increased openness, flexibility, and the reinforcement of a team approach. Large groups of workstations are divided into small neighborhoods by means of interspersed support areas that serve as a counterpoint to the regularity of the workstations. A sense of dynamism stems from the recurrent use of non-rectilinear forms.

Left, above: *Executive waiting room.*
Left, below: *Main reception area.*
Right: *Seating area with display panel.*
Below, left: *Executive conference room.*
Below, right: *Team area.*
Photography: *Dan Cunningham.*

Greenwell Goetz Architects, PC

Wellspring Resources
Bethesda, Maryland

Below: *Main reception area.*
Right: *Employee lounge.*
Right, below: *View towards administrative areas.*
Photography: *Jon Miller, Hedrich-Blessing.*

The design concept for this Florida-based software development company specializing in human resource management software was to provide a space that projected an image of an energetic and youthful corporate culture. With 68,000 square feet of space over three floors, a large number of workstations and support areas were to be efficiently laid out within a very irregular floor plan. To balance the box-like squareness of the stations every drywall in the space is angled and wooden door entries are canted. The use of vertical blind glass for the angled corners of private offices allows for changing non-static views of the interiors. The color palette is warm and light, with a metallic duroplex finish highlighting each team support grouping. Particular attention was paid to lighting. Because of heavy computer use by the staff, indirect non-glare lighting was provided for the workstations. Metal ribs of light in the corridors and public spaces help to project the high-tech image of the firm, while giving additional texture and play to spatial planes. The overall effect is of a dynamic and vibrant place to work.

Greenwell Goetz Architects, PC

NASA Auditorium
Washington, DC

This 250-seat auditorium for the National Air and Space Administration (NASA) has presented NASA officials with a more appropriate setting to conduct their meetings and presentations. It is a state-of-a-art facility, providing for rigid rear-screen projection, a direct downlink for NASA satellites, and direct connection to a video studio. A wavelike undulating ceiling with invisible suspension systems is designed to flow over the entire seating area. The perforated aluminum canopy is contoured to meet exacting acoustical requirements. A curvilinear light batten running through the central spine of the wave, together with a series of perpendicular battens, provides total flexibility for the focusing of lights throughout the space. Awards for the design have come from the General Services Administration's Public Building Services, the American Institute of Architects, the International Interior Design Association, and Interior Design Magazine.

The Hillier Group

500 Alexander Park CN 23

Princeton

New Jersey 08543-0023

609.452.8888

609.452.8332 (Fax)

Philadelphia

New York

Washington

Clarks Summit

Kansas City

Dallas

Sydney

The Hillier Group

Berlitz International Corporate Headquarters Princeton, New Jersey

Berlitz International is the premier worldwide language services firm. For its new Princeton, NJ, headquarters, it asked The Hillier Group to design 70,000 square feet of space, including a Language Center franchise prototype on the ground floor and three floors of offices above. The site is accessible by foot from the train station for New York and Philadelphia commuters, and services provided here include language and cultural training, translation services, and product publishing. The important Japanese component of the international company was subtly emphasized with a spare, simple design featuring shoji-like translucent screens. In the predominantly open-plan scheme, these panels provide privacy while admitting light.

Similarly, tall curved screens with asymmetrically placed openings provide more privacy without blocking spatial flow. Construction was accomplished in five months and cost $2,270,000.

Opposite, above:
Curving walls act as
privacy screens.
Opposite, below: a
pair of work stations.
Above: Translucent
screens divide space.
Right: Another worksta-
tion configuration.
Photography: Barry
Halkin.

The Hillier Group

Bell Atlantic Corporation
Corporate Headquarters
Philadelphia, Pennsylvania

The 235,000 square-foot headquarters of Bell Atlantic occupies the top 14 floors of the 51-story Bell Atlantic Tower in downtown Philadelphia, commanding striking views of Center City. For its design, The Hillier Group was guided by a recently adopted corporate mission statement emphasizing the "intelligent network" by "making communications simple again." To this end, an environment was created with few private offices and a high degree of visual openness, reducing physical barriers to increase interaction and communication between management and staff as well as between Bell Atlantic and the public. Participation by the public is focused on two unusual 50th-floor facilities, both double-height and ringed with mezzanines. One of these is the "Elevations Cafe," an upscale public cafeteria; the other is "The Forum," a technologically advanced auditorium for both internal and community use. The latest technology is also at work in the multiple-phone-line wiring of the workstation clusters, and in the zoned HVAC system serving all floors with individual controls. The installation is the winner of a design award from the American Institute of Architects, Philadelphia chapter.

Above: Corridor with art work and view into meeting room.
Right: "The Forum" auditorium space.
Photography: Matt Wargo © 1992, all rights reserved.

Above: *General view of the double-height "Elevations Cafe."*
Right: *Parapet detail.*

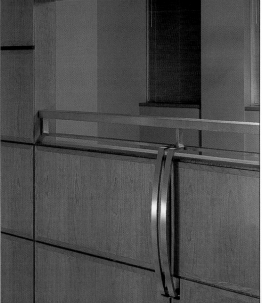

The Hillier Group

Deloitte & Touche
Two World Financial Center
New York, New York

Formed by merger in 1986, Deloitte Touche is one of the country's "Big Six" accounting firms. This 375,000 square-foot installation occupies eight and a half floors of a tower in downtown Manhattan. Its goal: to reflect the reordering of the firm's professional structure, now organized by market segment (entertainment, healthcare, etc.), rather than by function (taxes, audits). The businesses being served are thus emphasized, rather than internal divisions, and accessibility is the new keynote. The public, however, is channeled primarily to three "client floors," connected with one another by an open stair. Here are the boardroom, a wood-paneled library, interview and video conferencing rooms, a 150-person conference room, and a host of training facilities. On other floors, partners' offices have been reduced to 150 square feet, but are handsomely and effi-ciently outfitted with generous built-in storage in a custom wall grid of mahogany and anigré. Custom furniture is modular and flexible. Total construction cost was $28 million.

Above: Reception desk at entrance.
Below: View into lobby from the eighth floor.
Photography: Jeff Goldberg/ESTO © 1995, all rights reserved.

Above: *View into boardroom.*
Below: *The partners' lounge, an amenity compensating for reduced office sizes.*

Above, left: Private office for Deloitte & Touche by The Hillier Group.
Above: Detail of movable storage unit.
Left: Library adjacent to boardroom.

IA, Interior Architects Inc.

350 California Street
Suite 1500
San Francisco
California 94104
415.434.3305
415.434.0330 (Fax)

Boston
Chicago
Costa Mesa
Dallas
Ft. Lauderdale
London
Los Angeles
New York
San Francisco
Silicon Valley
Washington, DC

IA, Interior Architects Inc.

United HealthCare
Eden Prairie, Minnesota

Right: *View down into dining room "village."*
Below: *The entrance to the "village."*
Photography: *Brian Droege*

Right: Looking towards the "village" from the "boulevard."
Below: View of library from the dining area.

This 155,000-square-foot installation for a health care insurance company takes full advantage of its locale, an existing two-story warehouse space. Cafeteria, dining room, and training areas soar the full height and participate in spirited references to an Italian piazza, complete with domestic-scaled building elements, towers, and an approach through a colonnaded boulevard. The boulevard, fashioned from shaped drywall, also serves as a primary circulation spine for the large areas of open office workstations. Other facilities for the 825 employees include closed offices, conference rooms, and lobby. Careful use of vibrant colors brightens the composition with minimal expense. In the double-height cafeteria, color accent spotlights give additional visual sparkle. IA performed space planning, interior architecture, and project management duties, and brought the job in on time and — at $35 a square foot — under budget.

155

IA, Interior Architects Inc.

Skandinaviska Enskilda Banken
New York, New York

For the New York headquarters of S. E. Bank, a Scandinavia-based international corporate bank, IA has designed a 35,000-square-foot floor accommodating 160 employees. Work areas here are as open and non-hierarchical as reason allows. Even the president requested an open work station; overruled by his staff, he occupies the single truly enclosed private office, but one equipped with large double doors that are open much of the time. Other areas share light and degrees of vision through gridded walls of frosted glass at eye level, clear glass above. A special enclave, with all its necessary requirements of cabling, cooling, and careful lighting, is a trading room with 45 positions.

Top of page: Glass wall separates open work areas from a vp's office. *Middle of page:* Reception area with custom-designed desk of maple and frosted glass. *Right:* The trading floor. *Photography:* Paul Warchol.

Also provided are a lunch room, mail room, data center, and separate entrances for the bank's two subsidiary enterprises. Client satisfaction? Claes von Post, president of S. E. Bank, USA, says "We have the ambition to function on the highest level, and we feel that IA has helped to create an office that meets our needs and conveys our message."

Above: Gridded glass wall along a corridor, looking towards reception area.
Below: The conference room with leather seating, glass-topped table.

IA, Interior Architects Inc.

Offices for IA, Interior Architects Inc.
San Francisco, California

On the 15th floor of a downtown San Francisco building, IA has designed quarters for its own local staff of 65. The 15,000 square feet hold reception area, main conference room, smaller conference/work rooms, private offices, and two large studio spaces. Perhaps most popular both with staff and with visiting materials reps is a room, entered without disturbing any of the work areas, that doubles as kitchen and resource library. A series of sliding glass doors maximizes visibility but allows occasional privacy. The space serves not only its obvious functions but also the secondary role of public relations tool, the office design, according to IA spokesmen, having been a deciding factor in several potential clients' decisions to hire IA for their own office design. Cost was $40 a square foot.

Above: Kitchen area and resource library.
Below, left: Corridor view back towards reception area.
Below, right: Presentation room (photograph by Beatriz Coll).

IA, Interior Architects Inc.

Sony West Coast Design Center
San Francisco, California

For electronics and entertainment giant Sony, IA provided programming, space planning, design, construction documents, and construction administration services, resulting in this 7,500-square-foot ground floor space in a loft-like building. Unusual requirements included a model shop for the production of realistic replicas of new Sony designs, a presentation "war room" for showing those designs, and a simulation room where people can be observed (through a one-way mirror) interacting with the same designs. Also provided were a reception area, studio space, private offices, kitchen, toilet room, and lockers. High-ceilinged spaces in the studio and elsewhere, combined with a desire for indirect lighting, brought the innovative solution of high-intensity parking lot lights installed "upside down." Overall, $50 was the cost per square foot.

Top of page: *Small seating group in a break area.*
Above, left: *Presentation room.*
Above, right: *Reception area.*
Photography: *Beatriz Coll.*

160

212.251.0656

516.883.4906

212.251.0659 (Fax)

516.883.4909 (Fax)

IDT Associates, Inc.

274 Madison Avenue, Suite 201   156 Main Street

New York   Port Washington

New York 10016   New York 11050

212.251.0656   516.883.4906

212.251.0659 (Fax)   516.883.4909 (Fax)

IDTAssoc@aol.com   smnarch@aol.com

IDT Associates, Inc.

Brouillard Communications
New York, New York

Below: The office of the Chairman.
Photography: Peter Paige.

Brouillard, a subsidiary of advertising giant J. Walter Thompson, is an integrated corporate communications agency specializing in advertising and public relations. For 85-100 Brouillard employees, IDT has designed 50,000 square feet of space in New York's Graybar Building, an H-shaped structure with a large core, low ceilings, and long corridors. IDT's duties extended to "fit factor" and space utilization studies, building analysis, and full-scope interior architecture and design services, including graphics and signage. In addition to the usual quotient of

private executive offices, open work areas, and conference rooms, there is a central MAC computer room used for desktop publishing and ad layout composition. The corridors necessitated by the building plan have been used as galleries displaying recent ad campaigns. The client reaction? According to Irene Hansen, Brouillard's Executive Vice President of Finance and Administration, "We achieved in spades the goal of increasing our facility's efficiency and improving space utilization. The overall feeling is very attractive and modern, bespeaking the appropriate image of our business, which is communications."

Top row, left: *Central MAC room.*
Top row, right: *Corridor gallery, looking towards reception room.*
Above, left: *View into conference room with awards wall on right.*
Above, right: *Conference rooms with movable walls.*
Right: *Main conference room.*

IDT Associates, Inc.

Dankner Eye Care
Baltimore, Maryland

Right: Reception room.
Below: Waiting area seating.
Photography: Ron Solomon.

Operated by Dankner Eye Associates, P.A., this eye care center in northern Baltimore specializes in pediatric opthalmology. That means kids. The children, tested for a variety of conditions, generally spend two hours per visit, and 40 of them are here on a typical day, all of them in an age group described as "examination adverse." Controlling their flow and keeping them amused while waiting were major design challenges. Most striking among the design firm's solutions is a color palette of vibrant primaries. Also employed are interestingly shaped and angled wall surfaces, an open ceiling grid with a view of the mechanical services above, durable finishes such as vinyl wall coverings and birch veneer, and furniture groupings scaled for all ages. Functional requirements included multiple examination rooms, a pre-exam facility, a dispensing area, a cashier's area, a consultation and conference room, offices for the manager and comptroller, general office space with five workstations, and waiting areas for both adults and children. Total area is 4,000 square feet.

Right: *An examination room.*
Far right: *The cashier's area.*

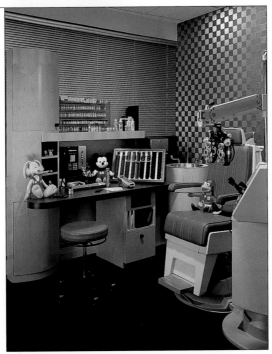

IDT Associates, Inc.

**Lever Brothers Company
Team Center
New York, New York**

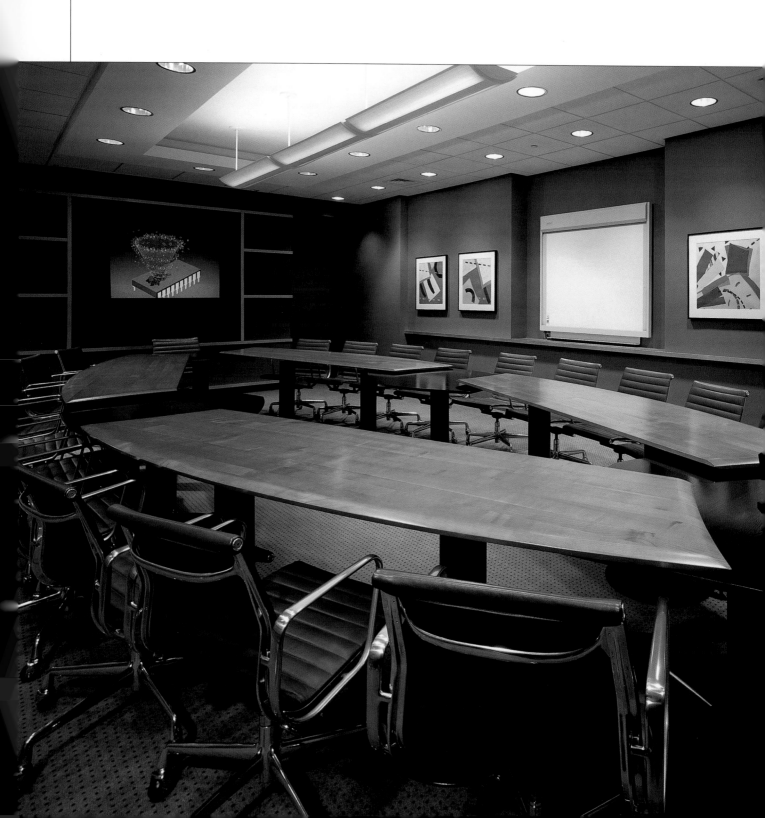

The landmark Lever House, on New York's Park Avenue, is as trim, sleek, and crisp today as it was when SOM's Gordon Bunshaft designed it in the early '50s. Inside that envelope, however, its interiors had become a bit dated. Lever Brothers, already an IDT client, came to the design firm with a request for a complete remodeling of the building's 17th floor into a "state of the art" conference center and executive suite. The building, of course, derives much of its effect from its radically slender floors, each offering only 6,000 usable square feet. IDT's ingenious solution to this rather tight fit gathers meeting rooms in an interior cluster (termed a "space capsule" by the designers) free of the perimeter walls. The clustering allows maximum flexibility in reconfiguring

Left: Small conference room with the movable wall in closed position.
Below: *Part of the data center.*

room sizes and shapes by means of movable walls, and the furniture is also easily moved and reconfigured. Clustering also permits a central service corridor serving all spaces with movable audio-visual and video conferencing equipment. Glass wall panels in metal frames, recalling the building's famous exterior curtain wall, admit light, but are frosted for privacy. The color scheme of blue and gray with gold accents is an IDT adaptation of the Lever Brothers logo. As further reminders of the company business, its consumer products are displayed near the reception desk.

Juan Montoya
Design Corporation

330 East 59th Street

2nd Floor

New York

New York 10022

212.421.2400

212.421.6240 (Fax)

Juan Montoya Design Corporation

The Offices of
Juan Montoya Design Corporation
New York, New York

On Manhattan's Upper
East Side, enjoying a
splendid view of the
59th Street Bridge and
the tramway to
Roosevelt Island, is the
2,500-square-foot, sec-
ond-floor studio/office/
showroom designed for
his own firm's use by
designer Juan Montoya.
A pair of custom-
designed bronze and
glass doors opens from
the public corridor into
the light-filled show-
room space, with a
receptionist's alcove at
hand. Beyond the show-
room, scene of frequent-
ly changing delights, are
a small kitchenette,
blueprint room, storage
room/library, four-person
drafting room, and pri-
vate offices for the firm's
two project directors
and for Montoya him-
self. This last space,
approached by a corri-
dor lined with marble
busts on pedestals, origi-
nally carved in the 1930s

***Opposite, and this
page, bottom right:***
*Two views of Montoya's
private office.*
***Other photos, this
page:*** *Three views of the
showroom space.*
Photography: *Billy
Cunningham.*

for an Italian garden, and alabaster wall sconces by French modernist Pierre Chareau, establishes the eclectic connoisseurship evident throughout. Here are combined a rosewood desk and antique chairs, a large contemporary mutimedia painting/construction by Manolo Valdes, a scuptured head by Igor Mitoraj, a gilt-framed, easel-mounted copy of an 18th-century genre painting by Jean-Baptiste Greuze. As a striking but recessive backdrop for such display, all ceilings have been kept their full 12-foot height with ducts and pipes frankly exposed, walls have been painted white, and the existing wood floors have been ebonized. Custom cabinetry is of maple.

Left: Entrance door and one of a pair of wall-mounted consoles.
Right: Corridor to Montoya's office, lined with Italian garden figures.

Juan Montoya Design Corporation

Niko Companies
New York, New York

Having a repeat client, according to Juan Montoya, "is the greatest indication of client satisfaction." In this case, the Montoya office had designed residences in both New York and Florida for Manny Kladitis, president and founder of the Niko Companies; Kladitis then returned with a request for similar services for his 25-person, 3,000-square-foot New York office. The business conducted here is that of theater production, so that a degree of theatricality was appropriate, but not enough to hinder in any way the functionality of day-to-

Left: View towards reception area from the desk of the president's assistant.
Below: Reception desk and visitor waiting area.
Photography: Billy Cunningham.

Above: *Office of Niko's president. Leather-top desk is a Montoya design.*
Right: *Detail of custom brass hardware.*

day work. Facilities provided include both private and open offices, reception area, mail room, conference room, and storage. Complicating the process was the fact that the office's former tenant, the Schubert Organization, was still occupying part of the space when construction began. The Niko move-in was therefore necessarily in stages, with new construction designed and timed to accommodate every phase. A neutral color scheme is spiced with natural cottons in a bright red, and other accent materials are maple and bronze.

Left, above: Open staff workstations for the Niko Companies.
Left, below: Desk of the president's assistant. Seating group in front of maple-paneled wall is used both for visitor waiting and for small conferences.

Working Spaces :
The Lauck Group

1800 McKinney Avenue

Dallas

Texas 75201

214.922.9000

214.871.3307 (Fax)

working.spaces@lauckgroup.com

Working Spaces : The Lauck Group

Pinnacle Brands, Inc.
Dallas, Texas

Pinnacle Brands is a young, progressive marketing firm, its present specialty being the creation and distribution of premium trading cards for major league sports figures. When its rapid growth required a move to larger quarters, however, the anticipation of future diversity led the client and design team to avoid sports cliches. A sculpture of "Casey at the Bat" does greet visitors as they step off the elevator, as do interactive videos and a popcorn machine, but the sports theme is decidedly understated. The 50,000-square-foot installation houses a staff of 150 on three floors, and facili-

Left, above: Reception area.
Far left: Elevator lobby with "Casey at Bat."
Left: Corridor.
Photography: Joe C. Aker, Aker/Zvonkovic Photography LLP

ties include private and open offices, boardroom, teaming areas, and break rooms. Encouraging interaction, many office walls are glazed and many office entrances are without doors. Graphics painted at office entrances add pattern and color, white walls are foils for brightly upholstered furniture, and the generally muted color palette of white, black, beige, and taupe is spiked with accents of vibrant color.

Top of page: *Main conference room and stair.*
Above: *A manager's office.*
Right: *Open office workstation.*

Working Spaces : The Lauck Group

Offices for a Fortune 500 Company
Irving, Texas

Before design was begun on new Texas offices for this global engineering and construction firm, there was a rare summit meeting of its senior executives from around the world, sharing ideas with The Lauck Group and with one of the country's leading change management consultants. Discussing the alignment of the firm's expansive international facilities with its business vision led to the concept of creating "virtual headquarters" in diverse locations in Europe, Asia, and the United States. These were all to be highly functional, of course, but were also to be site specific, reflecting the host countries' culture, customs, and business climates. The facility in Asia, for example, was designed in accordance with the principles of Feng Shui, the ancient Chinese art of placement. The Texas headquarters illustrated here serves 10 local employees plus occasional "touch down" visitors and occupies 3,000 square feet. Some offices are private, some open; some permanently assigned, some available as needed on the "hotelling" principle. Prominent materials are pear wood veneer, textured loop carpeting, and frosted glass in clear aluminum frames.

Left, above: *Lobby.*
Left: *Entrance.*
Photography: *Joe C. Aker, Aker/Zvonkovic Photography LLP*

Left: *View into private office.*
Below, left: *"Hotelling" area.*
Below, right: *Corner of conference room.*

181

Working Spaces : The Lauck Group

Offices for a Corporate Client
Dallas, Texas

The client is a world-class organization in the software development business, and The Lauck Group is currently working on projects for the company in California, Paris, London, Amsterdam, and Dusseldorf. The headquarters seen here, however, is in a premier Dallas location with remarkable views of the city skyline. A hundred employees are accommodated here on two floors of 20,000 square feet each and a third floor of 10,000, all connected by a graceful spiral stair. Every high-tech convenience and capability was to be present, but not visible. In the conference rooms, for example, the latest technological advances in multi-media presentation and video conferencing, along with special marker boards and flip charts, are all contained in custom mill-work. Conference tables and desks discreetly provide electrical, data, and phone capabilities for laptop computers. Full-service kitchens and serving areas are hidden near the conference and dining rooms. Spaces are varied with barrel vaults, domes, and coffered ceilings, and the detailed lighting plan highlights the client's art collection. Other luxe materials and finishes include handpainted linen wall coverings, figured walnut desks with limestone transaction surfaces, walnut parquet flooring, and hardware of pewter and bronze.

Above, right:
Administrative area.
Right: *Executive office.*
Photography: *Joe C. Aker, Aker/Zvonkovic Photography LLP*

Top of page: *Executive dining room.*
Above: *Seating area.*

Left: *Main reception area with spiral stair.*
Left, below: *Two views of the president's office suite.*

Lehman |Smith |Wiseman
Associates . LLC

1150 Eighteenth St. NW

Suite 350

Washington, DC 20036

202.466.5660

202.466.5069 (Fax)

Lehman | Smith | Wiseman Associates . LLC

Kirkpatrick & Lockhart LLP
Law Offices
Washington, DC

The 98,000-square-foot Washington office of this Pittsburgh-based law firm is located within the capital's embassy district. It occupies a below-grade level, where support services are housed, and five levels above grade. A conference center and the firm's law library occupy the high-ceilinged ground floor and establish a strong presence in the building lobby. To take advantage of the balcony views, the most public spaces, such as the reception area, have been located on the second floor. The reception area's great curving wall of Indian rosewood, detailed with polished stainless steel bars, is recalled in furniture shapes and finishes throughout the project. The receptionist's desk is also a curved rosewood form. The custom rosewood table has a platinum leaf top, and the custom carpet is bordered with black terrazzo with inlaid strips of zinc. Other prominent materials are high-gloss lacquered wood and panels of patterned glass. Thomas F. Cooney, III, a partner in the law firm, praises "an environment that is professional, comfortable, and consistent with Kirkpatrick & Lockhart's sense of itself."

Right: *View into conference room from reception area.*
Below: *Caucus room for private conversations is between two conference rooms.*
Photography: *Jon Miller, Hedrich-Blessing.*

186

Right: Reception area detail with black terrazzo floor.
Far right: Reception area with curved rosewood wall.
Below: Library with rosewood panels at ends of shelving units.

Lehman | Smith | Wiseman Associates . LLC

Federal Realty Investment Trust
Corporate Headquarters
Rockville, Maryland

Below, left: Typical office with view into atrium.
Photography: Jon Miller, Hedrich-Blessing

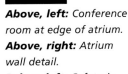

Above, left: Conference
room at edge of atrium.
Above, right: Atrium
wall detail.
Below, left: Cafeteria.
Below, right: Reception
area.

Because the client's primary business is the purchase and redevelopment of underutilized strip retail centers, it was natural that its new offices be a case study for such re-use. The 60,000-square-foot facility converts 35,000 square feet of poorly located retail space and adds 25,000 square feet of new space, with old and new wings facing each other across a newly created atrium. The skylit atrium, 20 feet wide and 200 feet long, serves as access to all administrative departments and functions. Offices overlooking the atrium have been given a degree of privacy by bamboo screening. Within the office plan, executives are housed within gypsum board enclosures 7 feet 6 inches tall, and support staff within open office systems furniture. To accommodate growth and change, all mechanical, electrical, and plumbing components are exposed and accessible. Flooring is natural cleft blue slate and exposed colored concrete. Ceilings are painted gypsum board and acoustical panels. Custom cabinetry is of maple veneer. In the office's present configuration, a staff of 120 is accommodated.

189

Lehman | Smith | Wiseman Associates . LLC

United States Olympic Training Center
Colorado Springs, Colorado

This 300,000-square-foot project on 35 acres has many components and was accomplished in three stages. Master planning began in the summer of 1987 and was finished by the end of that year. For Phase I, consisting of site work, a gymnasium accommodating 11 sports, and an aquatic center with a 25-by-50-meter pool, design was begun in March, 1991, and construction completed in October, 1993. For Phase II, consisting of further site work, a circulation spine called the Olympic Path, a Sports Medicine and Science Center, an Athlete Center, and a Visitor Center, design was begun in June, 1994, and construction completed in April, 1997. The 25,000-square-foot Visitor Center, seen below, is the primary support facility that serves the public, providing information about the United States Olympic Training Center and about the United States Olympic movement. Building elements and corridors have been planned to take maximum advantage of the site's Rocky Mountain views. There is a gift shop and café, an explanatory film is shown in the 225-seat auditorium, and separate exhibits feature Olympic medalists and athletes who have trained for the Olympics without earning medals. A drum-shaped exhibit hall, the building's most prominent volume, houses the U.S. Olympic Hall of Fame. The hall is topped with a skylight that affords a view of the Olympic Flame, held aloft by a steel tower and serving as the symbolic heart of the complex.

Above: *View of dining area.*
Left: *Within the display drum, the U.S. Olympic Hall of Fame.*
Below: *A plaster cast figure lifts an Olympic torch.*
Right: *Fin wall seen at dusk.*
Photography: *Jon Miller, Hedrich-Blessing.*

190

Top of page, left:
Athlete Center dining
with "elbow bar."
Top of page, right:
Athlete Center check-in
area and lobby.
Above, left: The interactive display "Who Are
Our Athletes?"
Above, right: View of
main visitor information
desk from exhibit
corridor.

Leotta Designers Inc.

601 Brickell Key Drive

Suite 602

Miami

Florida 33131

305.371.4949

305.371.2844 (Fax)

leotta@bridge.net

Leotta Designers Inc.

Ryder System Inc.
Miami, Florida

Right, above: *Cafeteria food service area.*
Right, middle: *The general seating area in the cafeteria.*
Right, below: *The receptionist's custom-designed desk.*

The design motif of the wheel seemed a natural expression of the client's business, transportation logistics. Circular forms are therefore repeated throughout the design in plan forms and in details such as desks, sconces, and frosted glass accents. The scope of work here was the refurbishment of 20-year-old spaces comprising reception area, lobbies, a cafeteria accommodating a staff of 1,500 employees, and an adjoining servery. In addition, all these heavily used spaces had to remain functioning during construction. Miami's mild climate helped here, however, by permitting outdoor dining much of the time. The lobby and reception spaces were also related to the client's product by means of partitions that display illuminated transparencies of the services Ryder offers. The results: markedly increased use of the redesigned cafeteria, a much more positive impression on visitors, and a much closer relationship between the client company and its headquarters.

Leotta Designers Inc.

An Engineering/Manufacturing Headquarters
Philadelphia, Pennsylvania

For half the cost of a new structure, LDI transformed an old factory in suburban Philadelphia into a world-class headquarters for a manufacturing company and its 700 employees. The 250,000-square-foot facility, occupying two existing structures on a 40-acre campus, now contains a lobby, reception area, training center, general office space, conference center, customer center, and a showroom for the client's products. On floors as large as football fields, individual areas were given identity and visual interest by color coding and by placing furniture groupings at an angle. Vast spaces were punctuated with enclosed elements containing conference rooms and files, this strategy also allowing the re-use of existing file cabinets and shelving, thus concentrating available funds on more visible elements such as workstations. The angled layouts are complemented by turning the structure's many columns into multi-faceted accents. The reward for LDI? A cover story in a national magazine. In addition to the cost savings, the rewards for the client are shown here.

Right: *The executive reception area.*
Below: *Conference table and lounge seating in the president's office.*
Photography: *Tom Crane.*

Below, left: The product display center.
Below, right: The boardroom.

Leotta Designers Inc.

Harris Drury Cohen
New Headquarters
Ft. Lauderdale, Florida

Below: *A wall of plaster faces and hands presents the clients' trophies.*
Photography: *Nancy Watson.*

It could have been anywhere. The 23,000-square-foot floor in a mid-rise spec building of a suburban office park was nondescript indeed, yet the client, one of Florida's largest advertising agencies, wanted their guests to step out of the elevator and say "Wow!" Given carte blanche, the LDI design team combined fantasy with pragmatism. References to Florida's semitropical environment abound in such details as structural columns transformed into palm trees and a reception desk resembling a great coral reef. Outdoor furniture and live plants complete the picture. The agency's

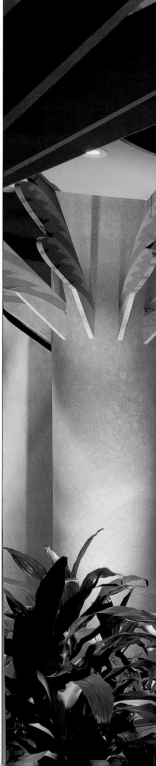

project/account teams are housed in a series of four "villages" clustered around a core of elements used by all the teams: resource center, art studio, and presentation rooms. Work areas and conference rooms only are carpeted, and ceiling tiles are omitted in many areas, giving the illusion of a high-ceilinged loft space.

Right: Another wall features the meshing of giant gears.
Below: Sheltered by "palm trees," the "rock formation" serves as the reception desk.

Each workstation has an acoustical tack panel for both sound absorption and creative urges. Near the "reception rock," surreal plaster hands project from the wall to offer visitors a look at the agency's collection of awards and trophies. Wow!

Left, above: *In a conference room, LDI has designed a multi-screen presentation wall.*
Left, below: *Where it happens: the ad agency's artists' studio.*

LPA, Inc.

17848 Sky Park Circle

Irvine

California 92614

949.261.1001

949.260.1190 (Fax)

LPA, Inc.

Kubota Tractor Corporation Headquarters
Torrance, California

At the request of the client, a Japanese tractor manufacturer, this West Coast corporate headquarters (totaling 30,000 square feet on two levels) and research and development center (75,000 square feet on one level) has a split personality. It was to have the appearance of being part of corporate America, yet it was to also express the company's Japanese roots. Japanese concepts and materials therefore appear throughout the complex, but in abstracted interpretations. A contemporary version of a Japanese garden provides a tranquil space between the office environment and the employee amenities facility containing a lunchroom and fitness center. The crushed stone of the garden continues inside the building, where it paves a display area for old, new, and prototypical tractors. Steel and glass interpretations of traditional Japanese shoji screens provide transition between spaces, and Japanese rice paper makes an appearance within sheets of laminated glass. Most abstract of all, the main boardroom is expressed as a great wooden cube "suspended" within the lobby atrium. Colors are warm white, deep, warm grays, and olive green, contrasted with the reddish-brown of the natural stone.

Opposite, above: *The reception desk recalls shape and materials of the building exterior.*
Opposite, below: *In the main lobby vintage tractors are displayed.*
Photography: *Adrian Velicescu.*

Top of page*: Main conference room "suspended" within entrance lobby.*
Above, left: *The corporate spine lighted by a 250-ft.-long skylight.*
Above, right: *View from lunchroom towards corporate offices.*

Lake Hills Community Church Chapel
Lake Hills, California

This 6,500-square-foot chapel seats 200 and is used for weddings, memorial services, and chamber music recitals. It is part of a 26-acre master plan that includes a gymnasium, fellowship hall, classroom buildings, and administrative offices. Traditional in plan but modern in form, the chapel blends well with its context, and the surrounding landscape design includes an English walking garden, shady oak trees, olive groves, and a memorial rose garden. The chapel design has won awards for LPA from the American Institute of Architects at several levels: the Orange County chapter, the State of Colorado, and the Western Mountain Region.

Brea Community Center
Brea, California

A focal point for the Orange County city of Brea, this facility is intended as a place where the community is invited to play, to learn, and to socialize. Within its 52,500 square feet is a multi-purpose room seating 300 (banquets being one of the purposes), a kitchen, an art studio, meeting rooms, classrooms, a family counseling room, areas for tiny tots and for teens, and a 12,000-square-foot gymnasium with showers, lockers, and aerobic and fitness rooms. The main reception counter is a highly visible focus for all parts of the building, and here staff can check in "wellness fitness" customers, answer visitors' questions, and generally oversee the building's activities. Beyond the reception counter, major activities are organized around a large, open central concourse; intended primarily as a circulation spine, it can also function for food service or overflow activities, and the after-school program uses it for ping-pong and other games.

Above, left: *Lake Hills Chapel.*
Photography: *Tim Hursley.*

Left: *Brea Community Center.*
Photography: *Tim Hursley.*

Tarbut V'Torah Community Day School Irvine, California

LPA provided architecture, interior design, landscape architecture, and graphic design for this community day school. When complete, the complex of eight buildings will contain over 60,000 square feet of program area and house 500 students ranging from kindergarten through twelfth grade. In accordance with the clients' desire that visitors be given "the feeling of being in Israel," the school has been designed as a metaphor for the city of Jerusalem. Four "educational villages" represent the Jewish, Moslem, Armenian, and Christian quarters of the old city, and these surround a campus quadrangle or "temple mount" for the school's most important activities. The chief building, which is used both as a synagogue and as an educational facility, is located on an east-west axis with its ceremonial bema facing east towards Jerusalem. The Orange County chapter of the American Institute of Architects awarded LPA an honor for this project.

Above: *Tarbut V'Torah School.*
Photography: *Adrian Velicescu.*

LPA, Inc.

Mossimo
Corporate Headquarters
Irvine, California

LPA provided site selection, space planning, architecture, and interior design services for this corporate headquarters of a fashion design company. Warehouse space occupies 164,000 square feet, and the adjacent office facility is 42,000 square feet on two equally sized floors. This facility contains corporate office space, executive offices and dining room, design studios, a graphics department, manufacturing space for the company's product prototypes, and a lunchroom for Mossimo's 180 employees. The basic design problem was the creation of a high-end "cutting edge" appearance within a typical lease space and also within a typical budget. It was also a priority to integrate Mossimo's unique creative process with the discipline of a busy corporate office environment. Further equirements were for a high level of flexibility, particularly in the all-important design studios. LPA's solution references the glamour of the fashion runway with elevated platforms, rows of mannequins, and theatrical draperies. Design worktables can be rolled easily to new positions, and draperies opened or closed for greater or less privacy. High ceilings in

Right, top of page: *Executive lobby area.*
Right, middle: *Guest telephone area at main lobby.*
Right: *Looking through design area towards executive offices.*
Opposite page: *Changing photo displays personalize the main lobby.*
Photography: *Adrian Velicescu.*

WORKSHOP

gene

Right: Looking through design area towards executive offices.
Opposite: Changing photo displays personalize the main lobby.

critical areas offer the luxury of space, and rich materials -- cherry wood, glass, and fine fabrics -- are found in interior details. Yet the overall design maintains strict budget control through the use of tilt-up concrete panel technology for the building shell and of industry-standard sizes and configurations for the interiors. The warehouse facility and the 13.4-acre site cost $3.8 million; the office building shell cost $1.8 million; and the interiors, including furniture and finishes, cost $1.2 million.

McCarthy Nordburg, Ltd.

3333 East Camelback Road

Suite 180

Phoenix

Arizona 85018-2323

602.955.4499

602.955.4599 (Fax)

main@mccarthynordburg.com

www.mccarthynordburg.com

McCarthy Nordburg, Ltd.

Cohen & Cotton, PC
Phoenix, Arizona

For a "boutique" litigation firm in downtown Phoenix, McCarthy Nordburg has designed 20,000-square-foot quarters that supply the desired aggressive, innovative identity. As a young firm, Cohen & Cotton needed to appear large and established, but on the relatively modest budget of $55 per square foot. An unusual elliptical reception area sets the tone, and the reception area and offices beyond connote sophistication without the traditional trappings typical of so many law firms. Other facilities include a mock court room, paralegal stations, administrative areas, and an employee lounge. Luxury detailing employs anigré wood and etched brass. The design firm provided space planning, a design development package including furniture specification and construction documents, and a full service interior program.

Above: The entrance rotunda.
Right: Reception area beyond the rotunda.
Below: Partner's office.
Photography: Mark Boisclair.

McCarthy Nordburg, Ltd.

Walsh America/PMSI
Phoenix, Arizona

This fast-growing pharmaceutical processing and research firm commissioned McCarthy Nordburg to design 125,000 square feet of office space on the six floors of a single-tenant Phoenix office building. The budget was $35 per square foot, and the time schedule was "fast-track." The result: richly detailed accommodations for a staff of 180, including an executive floor, offices both open and closed, a raised-floor computer room, lunchroom and more. Design dollars were focused on telling details such as figured anigré paneling and indirect lighting in serpentine ceiling coves, integral hardware for sliding doors, and custom cabinetry for audio-visual and teleconferencing equipment. The project has garnered awards from both the Illuminating Engineering Society and the International Interior Design Association.

Left: Executive floor elevator lobby.
Above: Executive reception area.
Right: Conference room.
Photography: Mark Boisclair.

213

McCarthy Nordburg, Ltd.

Cramer Krasselt
Phoenix, Arizona

A historic Phoenix building designed in the Spanish Colonial style for the Knights of Pythias is the venue for these interiors for an advertising and public relations firm. While many historical aspects of the original architecture are maintained, the new look is Spanish Colonial no more, but a chic blend of the elegant and the industrial, a quality rewarded with a Design Excellence honor from the International Interior Design Association. Elements of the eclectic but successful mixture include a wall of rotary ground steel, maple-clad bookcases, exposed brick bearing walls, and panels of sandblasted glass. Arched soffits and interlocking panels represent connectedness among the client's 55 employees. Total square footage is 16,000, distributed evenly on two floors, and the budget was $30. per square foot.

Left, above: Reception area utilizing industrial materials
Left, below: Boardroom, formerly the stage of the historic structure.
Right: Office corridor is the spine of the scheme.
Photography: Michael Norton.

McCarthy Nordburg, Ltd.

Walgreens Healthcare Plus
Tempe, Arizona

With lakefront view, these quarters for a pharmaceuticals manufacturing and distribution firm are in the Arizona State University Research Park. Totaling 85,000 square feet on two floors, the space combines a gracious public presentation with a no-nonsense, state-of-the-art distribution facility. More specifically, it combines high-end lobby areas with an adjacent warehouse. The materials palette includes stainless steel (for the reception desk), maple, and cherry. Colors are predominantly earth tones with accents in soft blue. The budget: $30. per square foot.

Above: *The adjacent conference room with view of lake.*
Right: *Reception desk and customer lobby.*
Photography: *Mark Boisclair.*

Mekus Studios Ltd

455 East Illinois Street

Suite 575

Chicago

Illinois 60611

312.661.0980

312.661.0778 (Fax)

Mekus Studios Ltd

Sanford C. Bernstein & Co., Inc.
Chicago, Illinois

Below: Reception area with conference room beyond.
Photography: Doug Snower.

Sanford C. Bernstein & Co.,

Right: Receptionist's
desk and waiting area.
Right, below:
Conference room.

This nationwide invest-
ment firm's Chicago
office occupies approxi-
mately 13,000 square
feet and houses 40
employees. The design
needed to present an
image consistent with
the firm's other offices
and appeal to its high-
end clientele, yet with-
out a large construction
cost. The Mekus Studios
solution emphasizes
spaces, such as the reception area and conference
room, that are frequent-
ed by visitors. These
spaces are enriched with
custom millwork and
with subtly stepped ceil-
ing planes created from
drywall. Private work
areas for the staff are
kept separate and utilize
more standard furnish-
ings and materials.
Between the two areas,
however, a maximum

amount of natural light
is shared by means of
glass sidelights and
clerestories. Throughout,
a major emphasis is
placed on the combina-
tion of natural and artifi-
cial light, to accentuate
the office's spatial organization.

Mekus Studios Ltd

Ameritech
Technology Control Center
Chicago, Illinois

Below: *Rotunda and viewing platform for the Operations Control Center beyond.*
Photography: *Jon Miller, Hedrich-Blessing.*

This 13,500-square-foot facility for telecommunications giant Ameritech serves two purposes: as an operations center and as a marketing tool. Its sophisticated technology performs essential functions, of course, but it has also been made visually accessible to visiting end-users, potential customers, and the public. This is work as theater. Two key areas, the Operations Control Center, which monitors all Ameritech's internal operations in a five-state region, and the Network Control Center, which displays the company's networking and communication capabilities, are visible through curved ceiling-high glass walls. From the public areas, a raised platform affords sweeping views of the work areas and their wall-mounted monitors. Particularly critical in this design was the lighting, which uses direct, indirect, and task fixtures in a variety of ways; special

Left: Operations Control Center with stairs leading to viewing platform.
Left, below: Technicians' workstations at the Universal Help Desk.

lenses minimize glare on the facility's many display terminals. Lighting has also been used to heighten the drama, a cold-cathode valance drawing attention to the rows of wall monitors and screens. The installation earned a design award from the Illuminating Engineering Society of North America.

Mekus Studios Ltd

SMG Marketing Group
Chicago, Illinois

For several years, SMG Marketing Group, a market research and software development firm, enjoyed quarters in a series of small brownstone buildings in Chicago's Gold Coast neighborhood. Moving to a 27,000-square-foot floor in the John Hancock tower, SMG wanted to retain some of the residential quality of that previous environment. The Mekus Studios response dedicates some of the space to the viewing of the client's art collection and also allows space for a number of congenial meeting environments; it uses curved wall planes, columns, detailed millwork, and "internal bay windows"

to create an eclectic, non-institutional character; and it employs a high degree of vibrant color to convey an impression of warmth and energy. Even so, a unity of effect is achieved by the consistent use of a single furniture system throughout, and costs have been contained by the use of

Right: Corridor with break-out area.
Below: Reception area.

Left: *Executive office with shared conference room in foreground.*
Below, left: *One of SMG's open-plan office areas.*

painted drywall, standard panel fabrics, and standard carpeting. John Henderson, president of SMG Marketing Group, says "We were very impressed with the professional and courteous nature of everyone" at Mekus Studios, and "I am very pleased with our new space."

Mojo•Stumer
Associates, P.C.

55 Bryant Avenue

Roslyn

New York 11576

516.625.3344

516.625.3418 (Fax)

Mojo•Stumer Associates, P.C.

Hewlett Packard
Huntington, New York

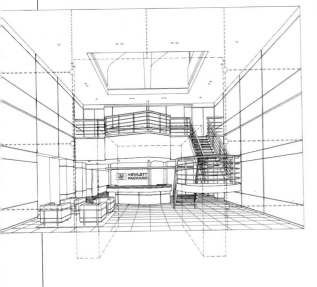

Winner of a design award from the Long Island chapter of the American Institute of Architects, this new freestanding building and its interiors were both designed by Mojo•Stumer. Encompassing a total of 200,000 square feet on two extensive floors, the facility accommodates more than 400 employees of the giant computer company. A wide range of facilities were provided, including a conference center featuring the state-of-the-art audiovisual equipment expected of such a company, much of it housed discreetly within a custom-designed wall of wood paneling. Client response? According to Mark Stumer, partner of the Mojo•Stumer firm, the architecture and design have been "a big hit" with the Hewlett Packard corporate office in California.

Above, left: *Perspective sketch of entry and front stair.*
Below, far left: *Reception desk.*
Below, left: *View of lobby.*
Photography: *Jennifer Levy.*

Above: Conference center with custom-designed wood wall.
Below, left: Exterior of building and entrance canopy.
Below, right: Profile of stair.

Mojo•Stumer Associates, P.C.

Dr. Jonathan Scherwyn
Offices
New York, New York

Dr. Jonathan Scherwyn, a successful plastic surgeon in Manhattan, required space for a waiting/ reception area, highly specialized rooms for treatments and procedures, and — most highly specialized of all —an operating room. All were to be housed within an existing space of 4,000 square feet. The space planning, according to the designers, "had to be very organized, using every inch of space." The result, necessarily, was a series of relatively small rooms with high ceilings. Capitalizing on the resultant prominence of the ceiling planes, Mojo•Stumer's design solution employs a virtuoso vocabulary of inter-

Above: View into a consultation room.
Right: Corridor leading to operating room.
Photography: Chris Wesnofske.

estingly shaped roomtop forms, all inexpensively constructed of gypsum board. Walls of rich wood paneling impart a sense of quality. Total cost per square foot, including furnishings, was $150.

Right: The doctor's waiting room, with reception desk beyond.

Mojo•Stumer Associates, P.C.

Olsten Corporation
Melville, New York

Olsten is a corporation engaged in the business of staffing other companies. The commission illustrated here involved the addition of a new three-floor, 75,000-square-foot extension to Olsten's exisitng 120,000-square-foot operation on Long Island. There were two obvious design challenges to the assignment: first, the aesthetic problem of blending old and new into a single cogent composition; and, second, the planning problem of constructing the addition with minimal disruption of the original facility. Both challenges were satisfactorily met.
The new element contains a spacious, image-conscious waiting and reception room, private offices, a cafeteria for the 450 employees, and a fitness center.

Mojo•Stumer's work, with Thomas J. Mojo acting as principal in charge, included architecture, space palnning, and interior design.

Below: Lobby area with reception desk and stair.
Right, above: Detail of the stair's handrail.
Right, below: Stair and waiting area beyond.
Photography: Mark Samu.

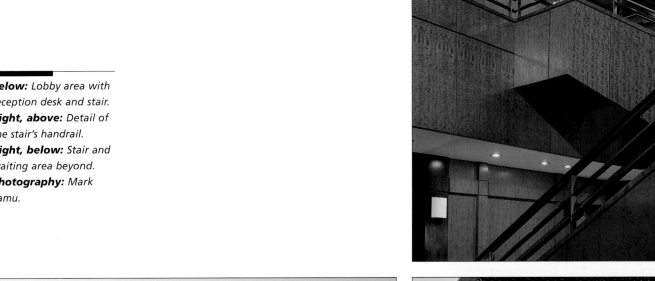

Mojo•Stumer Associates, P.C.

The Klockner Company
Garden City, New York

Mojo•Stumer's client, in this case, was a German-based importer of steel. This American branch of the company, located on Long Island, occupies a total of 45,000 square feet on two adjacent floors and, in addition to offices, contains a conference center and a lunchroom for the 165 on-site employees. Lobbies on two levels are connected by an elegantly detailed spiral stair. In those lobbies and elsewhere, prominent materials include black granite, wood paneling, and, not surprisingly, steel — in this case, stainless. Principal-in-charge for

Mojo•Stumer was Mark D. Stumer, and the cost per square foot was $125. The international client has expressed its approval, among other ways, by featuring the offices in its corporate brochure.

Left: Spiral stair, seen from elevator lobby.
Bottom of page: *The lobby's view of the reception desk.*
Photography: *Mark Samu.*

Montroy Andersen Design Group, Inc.

432 Park Avenue South

10th Floor

New York

New York 10016

212.481.5900

212.481.7481 (Fax)

Montroy Andersen
Design Group, Inc.

Mendelsohn Kary Bell & Natoli, PL
New York, New York

Right: *Typical private office with glazed strip near ceiling.*
Below: *View from elevator towards entry, reception, and conference areas.*
Photography: *Wade Zimmerman.*

This 12,500-square-foot installation for an accounting firm accommodates a staff of 40. Facilities include private offices, workstations, conference areas, a telecommunications room, and support and storage areas. A primary design challenge was to provide spatial variety within the office. Towards this goal, ceiling heights in the primary circulation loop, which doubles as a gallery, were dropped to eight feet, thus contrasting with the 9-ft.-6-in. Height of the reception area, main conference room, and private offices. The lowered ceiling also serves to house the technical requirements of the main HVAC trunk duct and sprinkler main. Another challenge was the provision of a lighting system that

would supply ambinet lighting throughout. Wall washers are effectively used in the private offices, and task lighting is added by means of reflected light and continuous torcheres at the workstation areas. Frank Lloyd Wright chair designs in the reception area established the Prairie School design theme, and principal materials are cherry wood, stainless steel hardware, drywall, and glass.

Above: *Main corridor which also acts as a gallery for client owned artwork. Wall planes, materials and lighting are designed to accept artwork and create a rhythm for the corridor.*

Montroy Andersen Design Group, Inc.

Fieldstone Capital Management
New York, New York

Fieldstone Capital Management is a firm of private capital investors and financial managers. For their 20,000-square-foot offices on two floors, they wanted a clean, well defined separation of public and private spaces, a separation effected with what the designers term "hard" and "soft" divisions. A "hard" division is a feature wall between reception area and back office; more "soft" distinctions are made by such subtle devices as the manipulation of ceiling heights. Among the spaces with more expansive heights are the open workstation areas, which "breathe" with activity and interaction. The installation houses a staff of 60 for Fieldstone, and costs totaled $85. per square foot.

Below, left: *Play of solid and glazed panels.*
Below, right: *In reception and conference rooms, a "faux" painted wall penetrates a glass plane.*
Bottom of page: *Main circulation corridor between perimeter offices and interior workstations.*
Photography: *Paul Warchol.*

Montroy Andersen
Design Group, Inc.

I/B/E/S International, Inc.
New York, New York

Located on the 18th floor of One World Trade Center in Manhattan, these 30,000-square-foot quarters house I/B/E/S International, a 200-person firm engaged in business information analysis and reporting. Prominent among the design problems here was the creation of a sat-

isfactory promenade linking the elevator lobby, buried deep in the building's core, to the I/B/E/S offices along the perimeter. This promenade, marked by cherry-faced columns and indirectly lighted, presents a series of corporate logos to the arriving visitor. At the end of the colon-

nade is the reception desk, a curved feature wall, and an adjacent conference room. The installation also includes a 1,200-square-foot data center.

Below, left: Reception area and adjacent glass-walled conference room.
Below, right: Entry corridor with a colonnade of cherry wood pillars.
Photography: Paul Warchol.

237

Montroy Andersen
Design Group, Inc.

ITG Boston
Boston, Massachusetts

Left: Perimeter offices' custom glass wall matches the historic building's window details.
Below: Workstations detailed with wood, glass, fabric, and concealed lighting.
Photography: Wade Zimmerman.

ITG is a fully automated trading and securities firm that develops systems and software to help the trading community in electronically tabulating trades and stock acquisitions. The firm required a branch office in the Boston area to support a staff of 40 and a new "disaster recovery" communications room. Montroy Andersen's plan uses the communications room as the focus of the floor plan and distributes the branch office around it, thus affording many office views of the rows of modem racks and other impressive technology. Except for the

reception area and conference room, all parts of the installation are on a six-inch-high raised floor for the ultimate in flexibility. Aesthetics are far from neglected here, however, and the character of the historic building housing these offices has influenced interior detailing and materials. These last include cherry

Above: Reception area with skylight, cherry and anigré woods, marble flooring.
Right: Conference room detail. Table and credenza are of matched anigré panels.

and anigré paneling, patterned flooring of green marble, and elements of stainless steel and wood-framed glass. Two existing skylights add to the dramatic nature of the interiors, and the careful detailing throughout has earned Montroy Andersen an Award of Excellence from the Architectural Woodwork Institute.

Left: *Perimeter offices re-use the historic building's tall windows.*
Below, left: *Conference room.*
Below, right: *Ceiling planes are manipulated to help define work areas.*

O'Donnell Wicklund Pigozzi and Peterson Architects Incorporated (OWP&P)

111 West Washington Street

Suite 2100

Chicago

Illinois 60602.2711

312.332.9600

312.332.9601 (Fax)

www.owpp.com

OWP&P

University of Chicago Hospitals
Duchossois Center for Advanced Medicine
Chicago, Illinois

The 525,000 square foot Duchossois Center for Advanced Medicine, a new facility on the University of Chicago Medical Campus, opened on November 19, 1996. Its owners wanted an impressive ambulatory care facility that would provide quality care under one roof and support the Hospitals' mission to remain an institution of choice and competitive in the regional managed care market. Interior Designers at OWP&P met the challenge of creating a dignified, comfortable, patient-focused atmosphere that conveys values of tradition and importance. Architect of Record was HLM.

The Center's two-story atrium entrance features wood accents, stone materials, and a staircase made of bronze, glass and wood. These materials also used in the elevator lobby complement the campus' Gothic tradi-

tion. Warm lighting effects reinforce intimacy and humanize the scale of this awe-inspiring space, as visitors move from the entrance to waiting areas. These design elements strike a balance between elegance and comfort, maintaining the patients' positive experience throughout their visit.

Left: *Reception lobby with stair to mezzanine.*
Above: *Vaulted ceiling and cove lighting above elevator bank.*
Photography: *Steve Hall © Hedrich-Blessing.*

243

OWP&P

CNA Insurance
CNA Conference Services
Chicago, Illinois

A large insurance company with real estate holdings of more than a million square feet, CNA has commissioned OWP&P for a number of planning and design assignments. The one shown here is a 14,000-square-foot conference center. A system of movable walls provides maximum flexibility to the sizes and shapes of conference rooms, where high-tech audio/visual systems are supplied, along with 'phone stations for attaching conferees' laptop computers. In addition, the design serves to illustrate the client's corporate history. Red, CNA's corporate color, is the accent color throughout the conference center. For a prominent corridor, upon OWP&P's recommendation, CNA commissioned artist Stephen Knapp to produce eight 36-in. x 80-in. sculptured glass panels depicting the major buildings the company owns nationwide and the evolution of the CNA logo.
American sycamore has been used for custom millwork, and other materials include granite and stainless steel.

Above: Reception desk with elevator lobby beyond.
Left: Art glass panels by Stephen Knapp.
Photography: Steve Hall © Hedrich-Blessing.

OWP&P

Offices of OWP&P
Chicago, Illinois

Right: *Lobby with firm logo projected on floor.*
Below: *Stair connecting the 21st and 22nd floors.*
Photography: *Chris Barrett © Hedrich-Blessing.*

Consolidating a previously scattered staff of 255, OWP&P's new offices are on the top three floors of the 85-year-old Burnham Center in Chicago's Loop. The 59,000-square-foot facility also enjoys access to the building's roof garden. The process of searching for suitable space, then designing suitable interiors and custom furniture, was undertaken as a model of the designer/client relationship, with one group of employees designated the project design team, another designated the client representatives. OWP&P staff also provided structural and mechanical engineering and lighting, security and telecommunications systems design. The result: an upbeat, energetic environment that "looks like an architectural office."

OWP&P

Knoll International (Group)
Showroom and Offices
Chicago, Illinois

Knoll is highly respected in the design industry as a pioneering and progressive furniture manufacturer. In designing Knoll's new 6,000-square-foot showroom addition in Chicago's Merchandise Mart, OWP&P realized the need to reflect the client's commitment to quality and its emphasis on design. "Good design," as co-founder Florence Knoll is known for saying, "is good business." Another consideration was that the addition needed to provide highly functional office space while also displaying merchandise in the best light. Still another was that it have its own personality while seeming consistent with the existing showroom on the floor above. All requirements were satisfied by OWP&P's imaginative solution that employs gently curving, slightly translucent panels of stainless steel mesh to distinguish the workstation areas. These sweeping panels subtly suggest the protection of a grove of trees, and the nature metaphor is continued with references to clouds (other panels), an open field (straw-colored carpet of DuPont's durable Antron Legacy), moonlight through the foliage (fluorescent lighting above the mesh), and even starlight (the twinkle of MR16 fixtures). On a more practical level, open spaces beween workstations have been planned to encourage employee "teaming," and the palette of neutral colors acts as a quiet backdrop against which the furniture is effectively showcased.

Kimball International
Showroom
Chicago, Illinois

Kimball International is one of the world's largest and most prominent furniture manufacturers. OWP&P was recently asked to help in the relocation of its showroom space in Chicago's Merchandise Mart to the Mart's tenth floor. The 18,900-square-foot space needed to present a major presence and an appropriate image, of course, and, despite an awkward L-shaped layout, an impression of coherence. Towards these goals, the palette of materials and colors has been kept simple and consistent. Elements include white-painted walls, floor-to-ceiling screens of woven metal mesh that demar-

cate showroom areas without forming visual barriers, and carpet tiles laid throughout in alternating stripes of two closely coordinated patterns. Flexibility is gained by the use of track lighting and of wall panels that can also be moved along ceiling-mounted tracks. Working office areas, which must also display their contents to visitors, receive the same aesthetic treatment.

Partridge Tackett Architects

1617 JFK Boulevard

One Penn Center

Suite 900

Philadelphia

Pennsylvania 19103

215.567.3595

215.557.7984 (Fax)

Partridge Tackett Architects

Murray Devine & Associates
Philadelphia, Pennsylvania

This renovation of office space for a firm of financial advisors might more accurately be termed a recycling project. For, although the 7,500-square-foot plan left by previous tenants was completely reconfigured, some of the valuable materials left behind were salvaged and re-used. Most notably, the exotic veneer paneling was demounted, modified, and reassembled. Glass partitions were re-employed as well, and some furniture pieces were reconditioned and recycled. The result of Partridge Tackett's design, achieving plan efficiency while adhering to the modules of inherited components, is that Murray Devine was able to enjoy a substantially higher level of finish than its $55. per square foot budget would normally have afforded. Complementary new elements include a marble boardroom table, custom wood workstations and files for administrative assistants, and custom colored carpets.

Above: Mahogany paneled executive office.
Below: Receptionist's desk and visitor waiting area.
Opposite: Corridor between reception area and glass-walled boardroom.
Photography: Matt Wargo.

Partridge Tackett Architects

Right Associates
Philadelphia, Pennsylvania

With a very slim budget to work with ($34. a square foot), and with a rush schedule (only fourteen weeks from commencement of construction to move-in), Partridge Tackett was able to provide a world-class 26,000-square-foot corporate headquarters for a Philadelphia consulting firm. The staff of 80 needed separation from visitors to the training center, yet a single receptionist was wanted, the result being a split loop circulation plan. Materials include flooring of gray and green slate and carpet, indirect pendant lighting, dappled stucco wall panels, and detailing of American cherry. Cherry frames also distinguish light-transmitting walls of etched glass. The Partridge Tackett duties performed included programming, site selection, test-fit analysis, all stages of interior and furniture design, construction contract administration, data/ communications systems coordination, and coordination of that all-too-soon move-in. The client reaction? According to Right Associates president Joe Smith, "This is gorgeous!"

Above: Stylized
entrance establishes
horizontal motif.
Left: Glazed corridor
continues the motif.
Right: The corporate
boardroom.
Photography: Matt
Wargo.

Partridge Tackett Architects

WDAS FM Radio Station
Bala Cynwyd, Pennsylvania

WDAS is an urban pop FM radio station with an AM sister station. For its 40 employees and numerous visitors (including gospel music groups) it required the interior and exterior renovation of a free-standing suburban office building. The 8,000-square-foot ground floor now holds the public lobby, meeting rooms, management offices, programming offices, and sales offices, and a staff lunchroom. The 4,000-square-foot second floor, accessible by stair from the building entrance, contains a suite of glass-walled on-the-air studios, engineering offices, and the community room, this last being an over-sized studio-quality space that can be used for large group broadcasts. Naturally, acoustical controls required

WDAS is an urban pop FM radio station with an AM sister station. For its 40 employees and numerous visitors (including gospel music groups) it required the interior and exterior renovation of a freestanding suburban office building. The 8,000-square-foot ground floor now holds the public lobby, meeting rooms, management offices, programming and sales offices, and a staff lunchroom. The 4,000-square-foot second floor, accessible by stair from the building entrance, contains a suite of glass-

Above: Art establishes a music theme in the lobby area.
Left: Black marble panel with station signage makes a first impression. The stair beyond has polished chrome rails.
Right: Visual contact among the four studio/production rooms.
Photography: Matt Wargo.

255

Partridge Tackett Architects

Independence Foundation
Philadelphia, Pennsylvania

Forced to relocate from ornate quarters that had once been a private apartment for the Wanamaker family, this prominent Philadelphia charitable foundation wanted a recreation, as far as possible, of those historic interiors. Partridge Tackett responded with the renovation of 5,000 square feet in a center city high-rise that is traditional, comfortable and near-residential in character. Raised paneling and moldings have been applied throughout, some painted, some in mahogany. The reception desk is of crotch mahogany inlay with a marble top. Other features are mahogany floors, Oriental rugs, cut pile carpeting, French doors, and — at kitchen and toilet — ceramic tile. Incandescent downlights and wall washers enhance the domestic effect. Services performed by Partridge Tackett began with programming and site selection and included graphic design services such as the redesign of the foundation's logo.

Right: *Comfortable seating group and mahogany reception desk.*
Below: *Traditionally detailed corridor.*
Photography: *Matt Wargo*

256

Perkins & Will

One Park Avenue

New York

New York 10016

212.251.7000

212.251.7111 (Fax)

Atlanta

Charlotte

Chicago

Los Angeles

Miami

Minneapolis

Perkins & Will

Fallon McElligott
Minneapolis, Minnesota

The 18,000 square feet was smaller than this advertising agency's accustomed standards for the expected population of 80 employees, and the budget of $40. per square foot was hardly generous. Yet the design process here left the client with a smile and Perkins & Will with a bevy of awards. A key element was the custom-designed furniture, which not only was less expensive than marketed counterparts, but also provided the interiors with a distinctive, dynamic character. Architectural elements such as stairs, reception desk, and a variety of overhead planes also participate in the active spirit of the design. Principal materials are birch and hot rolled steel. Among the awards garnered are those from Monsanto, from the Halo/Metalux national lighting competition, from Interiors magazine, and from the American Society of Interior Designers.

Left: Reception/waiting area with display wall.
Right, top: Sculptural stair faced with birch.
Right, middle: Custom-designed workstations.
Right, bottom: Small conference/presentation room.
Photography: Dana Wheelock, Wheelock Photography.

Perkins & Will

Deloitte & Touche Consulting Group Chicago, Illinois

The radical remodeling of this two-floor, 40,000-square-foot facility reflects dramatic growth and an equally dramatic cultural shift towards alternative officing. The client, the consulting group of a "Big Six" financial services firm, has decided that most of its nomadic staff of 450 can best be accommodated in "hotel" spaces. Only the partners here have dedicated offices, and even those have been downsized from previous standards, the trade-off being shared conference rooms between pairs of offices. All others share open workstations, team work rooms, corner team tables and, along the windowed perimeter, drop-in work counters. These are all assigned temporarily as needed, with the help of a full-service concierge team. Materials prominent in the design are anigré wood paneling, birch flooring, glass, limestone, and Rosa Levanto marble. Indirect lighting has been used throughout to create a glare-free environment for laptop computers. The facility has established the benchmark for "hoteling" throughout Deloitte & Touche, with leaders from other offices frequently visiting, and with surveys showing the design "substantially exceeding expectations."

Opposite, above:
Typical "hotel" work
environment.
Opposite, below: Pair
of typical offices used by
partners or by teams.
Above: part of the conference complex.
Right: Conference
room. Millwork unit
holds A/V equipment.
Right, below: Detail of
interconnecting stair.
Photography: Jon
Miller, Hedrich-Blessing.

Perkins & Will

Coltec Industries, Inc.
Charlotte, North Carolina

After a 30-year history on Manhattan's Park Avenue, how does a company prepare its 85 employees for a move to a suburb of Charlotte, NC? The answer illustrated here is to hire Perkins & Will to design a working environment focusing on quality of life and providing the best in space, furnishings, lighting, and art. The resultant 40,000-square-foot facility, including private offices, boardroom, lunchroom, and library, has not only pleased the company's own staff, but also, according to Coltec Industries, "eased our assimilation into Charlotte." Design elements include dark woods, silk wallcoverings, a custom carpet in celadon green, and neutral backgrounds and special lighting for the art collection that is evident throughout. Perkins & Will interior design services included work with graphics, art, accessories, interior landscaping, and — of critical importance in this case — employee orientation. And all was accomplished on an accelerated "fast track" schedule, with only five months from design to move-in.

Left, above: A senior executive office.
Left: An executive office.
Left, below:
The chairman's office
Bottom of page: View from elevator lobby towards reception area.
Right: Beyond reception area, a corridor with a sculpture by Andrea Gill.
Photography: Marco Lorenzetti, Hedrich-Blessing.

Above: In the Coltec boardroom, a mahogany wall contains projection screen, sound system, and A/V equipment.
Above, right: Corridor view towards sculpture by Joel Perlman.
Right: Typical mid-management office. Print on wall is by Jasper Johns.

Quantrell Mullins & Associates Inc

999 Peachtree Street, NE

Suite 1710

Atlanta

Georgia 30309

404.874.6048

404.874.2026 (Fax)

Quantrell Mullins & Associates Inc

Smith Helms Mulliss & Moore
Greensboro, North Carolina

For their relocation into new four-floor, 70,000-square-foot quarters, this 70-year-old North Carolina law firm had some high expectations. Its partners wanted a traditional Southern environment but with progressive elements, fine materials but on a budget adhering to the

building's tenant allowance, new furnishings integrated with existing ones, and provision for future change and expansion. The design solution accommodates technology within a traditional setting. Attorney offices are on the perimeters of the floors, with paralegals,

secretaries, and support spaces within, and strict office standards with limited design choices allow maximum flexibility. The focal point of the scheme is a series of central rotundas linked vertically by a grand internal stair. The stair is open throughout the four floors, but cleverly con-

Below, left: Reception desk.
Below: Connecting stair.
Bottom of page: Rotunda with stair in background.
Photography: Brian Gassel.

Right: *Rotunda from stairwell.*
Below: *Reception room.*
Below, right: *Visitor waiting area.*

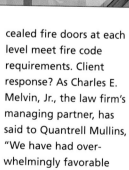

cealed fire doors at each level meet fire code requirements. Client response? As Charles E. Melvin, Jr., the law firm's managing partner, has said to Quantrell Mullins, "We have had overwhelmingly favorable response to our offices from clients, friends, attorneys, and staff. Thanks again for your professionalism and an outstanding result."

Quantrell Mullins & Associates Inc

Cousins Properties
Atlanta, Georgia

According to Thomas G. Cousins, chairman of this important Atlanta real estate development company, "All of us at Cousins are extremely proud and pleased with our new office environment. Your firm [Quantrell Mullins] did its usual outstanding job, and I am often told that our offices are some of the prettiest in Atlanta." Impressing arriving visitors immediately is the "Beaux Arts" layout of rotundas and gallery spaces that constitute the public areas. Because of the unusual building footprint of this new structure, these spaces enjoy from two

directions views of the surrounding national park. The display of the company's art collection is also a feature here, and there is access from these areas to executive offices, general offices, conference rooms, and the marketing center. Prominent materials here are polished marble, cherry and white lacquered wood paneling, linen and wool wall-coverings, and custom-designed rugs. Total area is 21,000 square feet.

Above: The chairman's office.
Right: Presentation/meeting room.
Right, below: Boardroom.

Quantrell Mullins & Associates Inc

First Union Corporation
Charlotte, North Carolina

The executive areas of the corporate headquarters of First Union Corporation, one of the 10 largest financial institutions in the United States, are housed on three floors of a Charlotte high-rise. First Union's presence in Charlotte includes not only many of the floors in this building but several other buildings as well. Quantrell Mullins was charged with planning and design of the 40th floor for executive offices accommodating 20 employees; the 41st floor for multi-purpose function and community meeting space for up to 400 people; and the 42nd floor, overlooking the lower levels, for the boardroom, board function areas and a portrait gallery. The large meeting space in the 70-foot high vaulted lobby on the middle floor includes sophisticated audio-visual and sound enhancement systems and fabric-covered ceiling panels to help control acoustics. Also evident are custom rugs, cream-colored lacquered panels, cherry paneling, silk wallcoverings, marble floors, and mahogany furnishings. Quantrell Mullins' services included space utilization studies, project budget and schedule development, programming and test layouts, space planning and interior design, furnishings design and coordination, furnishings selection and management, accessories coordination, cost and schedule tracking, bidding and awarding stages, construction administration, art program supervision, custom lighting, and, finally, move management.

Top of page: Part of the chairman's office.
Above: Another view of the chairman's office.
Below: View of the stair.
Photography: Timothy Hursley.

Left: *Lobby and stair.*
Below, left: *Executive reception area.*
Below, right: *The light-filled lobby.*

271

Top of page: First Union's boardroom waiting area.
Above, left: Executive waiting area.
Above, right: Administrative area.

Richard Pollack & Associates

214 Grant Avenue

Suite 450

San Francisco

California 94108

415.788.4400

415.788.5309 (Fax)

Richard Pollack & Associates

Charles Schwab & Co.
San Francisco, California

Below: *Waiting area with television/storage kiosk.*
Photography: *John Sutton.*

Serving 1,500 employees, this more-than-300,000-square-foot installation for a large financial company occupies 20 floors in five separate San Francisco buildings. Design challenges

included various trading floors, with their demands for power supply, cooling, ambient non-glare lighting, and proper computer monitor placement. Other spaces provided were private offices, boardrooms, conference rooms, computer rooms, switch rooms, training rooms, and employee lunchrooms. Client groups accommodated were Fixed Income, Bond Trading, Finance, Capital Markets, Annuities, Schwab 500 Trading, Asian Pacfic Trading, SITE, Schwab International, and In-house Advertising. Photographs shown here represent the Active Trading/Fixed Income and Annuities floors. In such a complex undertaking, well-organized floor plans and clear wayfinding indicators have been essential to occupant satisfaction and productivity.

Throughout, the designers have used "standard" materials — painted gypsum board, medium-density fiberboard, vinyl wallcovering — to create eye-catching shapes with texture and identity. Chief hues in the unifying color scheme are green and cream.

Left, above: Support service area.
Left, below: View into an employee lounge.

Richard Pollack & Associates

Fair, Isaac & Company
Regency II
San Rafael, California

Fair, Isaac is a world leader in risk management and the inventor of credit scoring systems used by financial institutions world-wide. Its employee population in Marin County, north of San Francisco, has been growing at nearly 22 percent a year for the past 22 years. Richard Pollack & Associates has continued a seven-year relationship with Fair, Isaac with this latest project. Called Regency II, it is a three-story building housing a staff of 375 in a total of 120,000 square feet. As a result of Pollack's post-occupancy evaluations of previous projects for the same client, and as a result also of worker surveys and workstation mock-ups, the new facility is a step forward in effectiveness and adaptability. Clusters of private offices ten feet square with adjacent support areas, meeting rooms, and storage space constitute interchangeable "repeating modules," which enable the client to maintain minimal disruption during its frequent employee moves. Extensive use of glass and open, informal "huddle" spaces encourage collaboration. These well-tuned office areas are supplemented by conference and teleconference rooms, training rooms, and a café with views of the rolling hills

Left: Curved reception desk and soffit above.
Right, above: Employee café.
Right, below: Office circulation with glazed office walls.
Photography: John Sutton.

Richard Pollack & Associates

CMP Media
San Francisco, California

Headquarted in Manhasset, New York, CMP Media publishes magazines and newspapers focused on computers, electronics, information technology, and the internet. For their new 125-person San Francisco branch, they chose a 25,000-square-foot converted warehouse with exposed heavy-duty concrete floors, mushroom-capped concrete columns, rough plaster walls and industrial steel window sash, and with a change of level splitting its single floor; not incidentally, it enjoys a dynamite view of the San Francisco skyline and bay. Needed in this raw space were a reception area, private offices, open workstations, lunchroom, conference rooms, and computer room. Richard Pollack & Associates retained the building's raw materials, exposed much of the newly added mechanical infrastructure, and placed a sculptural storage element along the line of level change, its shape recalling the form of the steel-girdered drawbridge seen from the

windows. The new elements, some in vivid accent colors, and newly added materials such as aluminum-framed glass and perforated stainless steel combine with the industrial shell to produce an office environment of uncommon energy and visual richness. Refined lighting elements add a final sparkle.

RTKL Associates Inc.

1250 Connecticut Ave., NW

Washingtion, DC 20036

202.833.4400

202.887.5168 (Fax)

www.rtkl.com

Baltimore

Dallas

Washington

Los Angeles

Chicago

London

Tokyo

Hong Kong

RTKL Associates Inc.

ACON Investments LLC
Washington, DC

RTKL's design for this 5,000-square-foot office for ACON Investments capitalizes on the unusually narrow space between the base building's elevator core and its perimeter. Because of the lack of depth, offices are organized along a spine at the perimeter, taking full advantage of vistas along Connecticut Avenue. To create a sense of openness within the confines of these spaces, the linking corridor has been edged with a glass wall that allows natural light into inner offices and pro-vides those offices with outside views. A serpentine wall undulates through the offices, offering varying degrees of openness and enclosure, adding fluidity to the spatial experience, and making a welcome departure from the typical straight corridor.

Right: An executive office, viewed through a glass partition.
Below: Conference room.
Photography: Maxwell MacKenzie.©

282

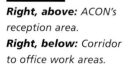

Right, above: ACON's
reception area.
Right, below: Corridor
to office work areas.

RTKL Associates Inc.

Computer Sciences Corporation
Executive Briefing Center
Fairfax, Virginia

Left, above: Main gallery showing private phone rooms.
Left, below: Executive briefing room with video conferencing and multimedia capability.
Above: Reception stair.
Photography: Maxwell MacKenzie.©

Left: *Entry into executive briefing room.*
Center: *Multi-media auditorium.*
Below: *Executive dining room*

As part of the 263 acre campus for Computer Sciences Corporation's Northern Virginia headquarters, RTKL designed a 44,000 square foot Executive Briefing Center. The principal challenge was to create a showpiece facility that can be used for marketing the company's world wide services while maintaining state of the art presentation systems. The task was to develop a design that supported the interaction of people and the use of technology as a tool for problem solving, while protecting the versatility and sustainability of the space.

The Executive Briefing Center houses facilities for training, demonstration, long distance learning and social functions through the use of digital multimedia, video-conferencing, and triple image rear screen projection. The interaction of clients and CSC employees is reinforced through the use of a central gallery and promenade that provides access to briefing rooms, dining, demonstration and auditoriums. Spaces for the company's internal functions are located separately, and never cross the galleries.

The spaces in the Executive Briefing Center are so versatile that they can function as video conferencing

rooms, executive presentation rooms or as high end work spaces for senior executives and their staff to close multimillion dollar transactions. Power, data and video connections used during groupware sessions or presentations are concealed yet accessible. Lighting systems provide for video conferencing through the use of high output indirect light from a suspended lacquered millwork trellis and point source accent lighting for presentation modes.

RTKL Associates Inc.

Coopers & Lybrand
Washington, DC

Above: *Reception area, with elevator lobby beyond.*
Left: *A partner's office.*
Photography: *Paul Warchol.*

The accounting firm of Coopers & Lybrand was intent on having a strong presence in the Washington area. In this design by RTKL, over 300 employees of the firm's national tax, financial advisory services, and other general practice groups now occupy 48,000 square feet in an office building in downtown Washington. To

Above, left: *Typical office corridor with accent wall.*
Above, right: *Main conference room with video and multimedia.*
Left: *Administrative assistant workstations.*
Below, left: *Typical manager's office.*

improve the efficient use of the space, a "hoteling" or office-sharing design was implemented. When not traveling or serving clients on-site, "non-territorial" employees log in at a central electronic kiosk and are assigned an available workstation, directed there by a map on the kiosk. Computer, voice mail, and telephone connections are then automatically routed to the proper location. The workstations are outfitted with docking stations for portable computers and other office equipment. Throughout the space, feature walls are highlighted with varying colors and textures to help orient the hoteling employees. Other materials and features include stone floors in the public areas, wall panels of anigré veneer, shaped plaster ceiling planes, and, for maximum light transmission, walls and side lights of translucent textured glass.

RTKL Associates Inc.

Goethe-Institut
Washington, DC

The Goethe-Institut is an international non-profit organization whose work abroad is funded by — but independent of — the German government. Its mission is to foster knowledge and understanding of the German language and culture and to contribute to international understanding and cultural cooperation. The Washington, DC, facility is one of 170 such institutes in 80 countries around the world. RTKL provided interior architectural services for the 7,000-square-foot space. Located on three levels of a renovated historic building in the downtown arts district, the new facility includes exhibition space, administrative offices, a classroom, and an auditorium seating 100 for lectures and presentations.

Above, left: Reception desk with conference area beyond.
Above, right: Detail of the reception desk.
Left: Lobby and stair.
Photography: Maxwell MacKenzie.©

SCR Design
Organization, Inc.

305 East 46th Street

New York

New York 10017

212.421.3500

212.832.8346 (Fax)

mail@scrdesign.com

www.scrdesign.com

SCR Design Organization, Inc.

National Academy of Recording Arts and Sciences
New York, New York

Below: Etched glass logo over a corner of the custom reception desk.
Photography: Paul Warchol

The National Academy of Recording Arts and Sciences (NARAS) is internationally known for the Grammy Awards it sponsors. It is an organization of more than 10,000 diverse members ranging from classical musicians to Rap performers, music producers, and recording specialists, so its headquarters space, seen here, needed to appeal to a variety of tastes.

Although relatively small (2,500 square feet), the office also needed to accommodate offices and both large and small spaces for meetings and receptions. Also needed was a research library where members can access either the academy's collection of compact disks or its information database.

SCR's design solution creates an appropriately contemporary impression. A strong sense of drama comes from the use of contrasting materials: black granite, white travertine, and custom millwork of pearwood. There are geometric contrasts as well in the theme of circles and squares, as in the custom carpet pattern. The circular NARAS logo is repeated throughout the installation in such elements as stone paving and etched glass panels, and, in the conference room, circular panels of perforated aluminum embellish the cabinet of audiovisual equipment.

Above: *Entrance foyer with reception desk and view into meeting room.*
Left: *The NARAS meeting room.*

SCR Design Organization, Inc.

SCOR U.S. Re-Insurance
New York, New York

Below, left:
The reception area.
Below: *Informal small
conference area.*
Photography: *Mark
Ross.*

SCOP U.S. is a re-insurance firm with a French parent company. Its United States headquarters was Texas and grew to two locations in downtown Manhattan. Beginning with comparative space studies for possible consolidated locations, SCR Design Organization determined that 57,000 square feet on two connecting floors of the Two World Trade Center building would be most appropriate. Alternative planning concepts were fully investigated, but the final scheme employs the more traditional concept of perimeter offices and interior workstation clusters. The private offices, however, have been fronted with glass partitions for maximum transmission of light and views. Within a white architectural shell, cabinetry, furnishings, and column covers of cherry make a striking impression, as do decoratively handpainted convex wall elements. These curving forms mark special areas and serve as focal points at the ends of corridors.

Pylon punctaute the reception area and connecting stairs. Similarly, important intersections in the circulation plan are accented by areas of travertine flooring. So pleased has the client been with the results that SCR was asked to work with SCOR on their Illinois acqusition company, thus establishing a new corporate standard for planning and design.

Above: Boardroom reception area, with view into an executive office.
Right: Connecting stair and one of the distinctive pylons.

293

SCR Design Organization, Inc.

Giro Credit Bank
New York, New York

Giro Credit now known as ERSTE Bank is a Vienna-based bank with multiple locations around the world. In relocating its New York office to expanded quarters on New York's Park Avenue, it wanted an elegant yet understated appearance that would be efficiently planned and cost-conscious. SCR responded with the design shown here, featuring wood-paneled walls, curved soffits and articulated ceiling planes in the public spaces, circular columns, and elliptical frosted glass wall sconces and pendant fixtures. All is strikingly offset by the use of dark carpeting throughout,

Left: Corridor with part of the client's black and white photography collection.
Below: private office with lounge and conference area.

and a collection of black-and-white photography turns corridor spaces into galleries. The reception desk, conference table, and other key pieces have been custom designed with exotic veneers and polished black granite. The installation totals almost 19,000 square feet and includes an up-to-the-minute teleconferencing room and a trading room accommodating 14 traders.

Settles Associates Inc.

1005 North Glebe Road

Suite 600

Arlington

Virginia 22201

703.525.0424

703.527.9263 (Fax)

www.settlesassoc.com

Settles Associates Inc.

New Carrollton Federal Building
Prince George's County, Maryland

Right: Cafeteria servery.
Below: Cafeteria dining area.
Photography: Anice Hoachlander.

The Internal Revenue Service has recently completed the transfer of 4,400 employees to this new headquarters complex in Prince George's County, MD, near Washington, DC. It is the result of a major General Services Administration design/build competition. Known as the New Carrollton Federal Building, the 1.2-million-square-foot campus consists of three nine-story buildings connected by pedestrian bridges and wrapping around a central green space. Operating 24 hours a day, the complex is virtually a small city. Its tenant-driven design developed by Settles Associates meets the IRS and GSA goals of integrating a productive workplace with an employee support network. To this end, space is divided into public, private, and service realms, with the public realm further subdivided into "neighborhoods." The

Left: The child care center's classroom and play loft.
Below, left: Training center.
Below, right: Auditorium.

largest of these, centered on a multi-story lobby, provides a variety of settings for employee education, including auditorium, training center, and library. Another, the "Main Street" section, contains cafeteria, snack bar, fitness center, and credit union. Still another houses family services such as the health unit and child care center. This last, a "village" within the "city," has its own simulated "street" with houselike façades and a child-friendly vocabulary of colors and shapes.

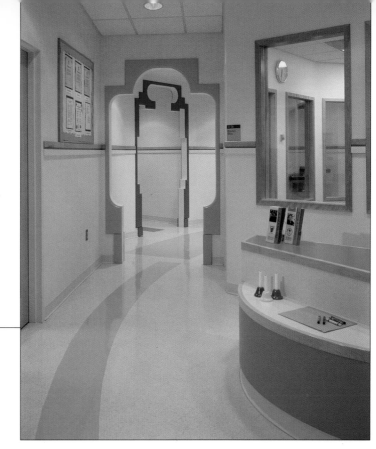

Right: Reception area, child care center.
Below, right: Child care center's "Main Street."

Settles Associates Inc.

U.S. Department of Health and Human Services
Health Care Financing Administration
Woodlawn, Maryland

Below: Executive presentation room.
Opposite, above: Auditorium.
Opposite below: Employee fitness center.
Photography: Alan Goldstein.

Settles Associates was selected in a General Services Administration competition to be a key part of the development, design, and construction team for the headquarters complex of the Health Care Financing Administration (HCFA), the federal agency that oversees Medicare and Medicaid programs. The winning scheme accommodates 3,300 HCFA employees in a 912,000 square foot campus which consists of three office buildings, a free-standing auditorium and a warehouse. The state-of-the-art facility incorporates a number of technically demanding special areas, including a 17,500-square-foot conference and training center, a multimedia room, teleproduction studio, tape editing room, satellite/earth station, uplink/downlink room, and a highly secure 34,000-square-foot data center. Also provided are an employee fitness center, full-service cafeteria, health unit, child care

Below: The Health Care Financing Administration's child care center designed by Settles Associates.

center, hearing rooms, and security control rooms. And, of course, plentiful office space arranged on large, highly flexible floors of 60,000 square feet, each served by a pair of cores. An accelerated schedule asked that the time from schematic design to completion of construction be only 32 months, so that the design of the building interior was undertaken while the base building design was still in development. All schedules and budgets were successfully met.

Silvester Tafuro
Design, Inc.

50 Washington Street

South Norwalk

Connecticut 06854

203.866.9221

203.838.2436 (Fax)

STDICT @aol.com

STDICT @compuserve.com

Silvester Tafuro Bishop

Design, Ltd.

25 Eccleston Square

London SW1V1NS

United Kingdom

171.932.0262

171.932.0797(Fax)

106615.3175@compuserve.com

Silvester Tafuro Design, Inc.

Duty Free Shops
Delta Air Lines terminal 1A
JFK International Airport
Jamaica, New York

Below: *Circular ceiling cove before a series of small shops.*
Photography: *Peter Paige.*

A recent trend in airport retail areas is that they are coming increasingly to resemble upscale shopping malls. Following that trend, Duty Free International (DFI) has chosen Silvester Tafuro Design, Inc. to design their retail outlets in the Delta Air Lines facilities at JFK International Airport. The one seen in this spread is a free-standing 7,000-square-foot area in the airport's Terminal 1A. Here, four interconnected boutiques — a duty free shop, a Coach store, a Sony music store, and a news and gift store — are accessed through three dramatic rotunda

entrances. Common to all elements is the lighting and the flooring, a neutral-colored synthetic stone. Colored inserts in the floor identify individual boutiques; the news and gift store, for example, has inserts of forest green stone. Because the entire composition is freestanding within the terminal, it has no ceiling, and, in order to create a sense of ceiling definition, the space is ringed with fascias and soffits. For the Coach and Sony boutiques, Silvester Tafuro designed shells that accommodate each company's standard designs. In the other two boutiques, the firm designed display cases, finishes, and other details as well, the materials vocabulary here including sapele wood veneer, mahogany trim, and black granite countertops.

Above, right: *Circular rotunda defines one of the entrances.*
Right: *Duty free shop.*

Silvester Tafuro Design, Inc.

Duty Free Shop
Delta Flight Center
JFK International Airport
Jamaica, New York

Right: *A classically inspired fascia unifies a selling area.*
Below: *A cashier's station.*
Photography: *Peter Paige.*

Another installation at JFK International Airport for Duty Free International is this elliptical- shaped 4,000-square-foot space in the Delta Air Lines Flight Center. This space comprises a collection of specialty merchandise boutiques or kiosks offering cosmetics, fragrances, watches, liquor, wine, and tobacco products. Display cabinets are either wall units or freestanding pieces, and they are detailed in either cherry paneling or faux stone. The entrance area, at the center of the ellipse, is also highlighted by cherry display units and wall paneling. Uniting the entire space is the flooring, a synthetic beige limestone with a mahogany-colored granite border. A unique feature of the flooring design is a ribbon of juperano Colombo granite that winds through the space, anchoring the display cabinets and guiding circulation patterns. The design intent throughout is an air of sophistication matching that of the showcased products.

Right: A freeform ceiling plane adds movement to a long expanse of shop.

Silvester Tafuro Design, Inc.

Hudson News
Retail Stores
Nationwide

Silvester Tafuro Design, Inc. is currently responsible for the design of Hudson News stores across the country, as well as for stores associated with 11 aviation concession programs. The Hudson News retail outlets are of four general types: Hudson News & Gift shops which are newspaper, magazine, and book "supermarkets," Grandstand Sports shop, Kid's Corner bookstores, and Book Corner bookstores. The first of these is generally designed to be very "high tech," but recent remodelings of the 19 Hudson News & Gift outlets at Atlanta's Hartsfield International Airport, timed to be ready for visitors to the 1996 Summer Olympics, called for something more upscale, so a wood scheme was developed instead. It uses canted uprights, indirect lighting, stainless steel accents, and plush cut pile carpeting. Silvester Tafuro also developed the concept and design for the Hudson News line of sport shops, Grandstand Sports, where local sports memorabilia are sold. A lively, animated atmosphere prevails here, achieved with a combi-

Right: Grandstand Sports at Dallas's Love Field Airport.

Below: The Hudson News outlet at Hartsfield International Airport, Atlanta.

Photography for all installations: *Peter Paige.*

Above: Kid's Corner Bookstore, also in the Hartsfield International Airport, Atlanta.

nation of video walls, television towers, fiber optics, and neon. The Kid's Corner bookstores represent another new concept, first introduced at the Atlanta airport. Several elements of the other bookstores are incorporated here, with a playful spin added. Custom woodwork is painted in bright primary colors and accented with animal carvings and sunbursts. There are also playful printed carpet designs, child-scaled furniture, a colorful building block logo, and, over it all, an indirectly lit blue sky ceiling. Finally, the Book Corner Stores, which have been designed for airports in Atlanta, Dallas, Houston, Newark, and Baltimore/Washington, are designed to recreate a gentleman's library. They employ mahogany paneling, hand-carved moldings, marble flooring and table tops, and decorative lighting. Because of accelerated schedules, many of these Hudson News outlets have been completed in remarkably brief time spans from demolition to completion, some within a year, some in as short a time as five weeks!

Skidmore, Owings & Merrill LLP

220 East 42nd Street
New York
New York 10017
212.309.9500
212.309.9750 (Fax)

224 South Michigan Ave.
Chicago
Illinois 60604
312.554.9090
312.360.4545 (Fax)

One Front Street
San Francisco
California 94104
415.981.1555
415.398.3214 (Fax)

46 Berkeley Street
London W1X 6NT
United Kingdom
0171.930.9711
0171.930.9108 (Fax)

Skidmore, Owings & Merrill LLP

Financial Institution
New York, New York

Above left: *Glazed wall of a typical office lets others share the Manhattan view.*
Left: *View from reception area to board room.*
Above: *The library for the firm's senior executives.*
Photography: *Marco Lorenzetti, Hedrich Blessing*

Occupying a total of 50,000 square feet on two high floors of New York's Citicorp building, these offices for a rapidly growing investment firm demanded the utmost in flexibility. Working with the established grids of the building's structure, glazing, and ceiling mod-ules, the SOM designers have responded with a universal lighting plan and a system of demountable partitions. Office enclosures that are largely of clear glass and doors of both clear and etched glass give most work areas a sense of openness and a share of the unpar-alled views. The motivated staff works long hours in this environment, but their work is rewarded by — and their work spaces supplemented by — a number of on-site amenities: food service facilities offering breakfast-through-dinnertime food, meeting rooms both for-mal and casual, a library and magazine room, and a fitness center with changing rooms, lockers, and showers for men and women.

Skidmore, Owings & Merrill LLP

Chase Manhattan Bank Trading Facility
New York, New York

Having designed the Lower Manhattan landmark building at One Chase Manhattan Plaza back in 1960, SOM returned recently to insert new trading facilities into the tower. Two trading floors needed to accommodate 228 traders each, with all their requirements of space, computers, power, glare-free lighting, and the dissipation of generated heat, and infrastructure was also provided for the future addition of a third floor with another 228 positions. New generators were added on the tower's roof, served by new tanks and fuel lines, and the trading rooms were provided with Uninterrupted Power Supply, chilled water lines, cabling risers, and a new data center. A less technical — but equally important — requirement for such large areas was the maximizing of ceiling height, a problem made more difficult by the need for six-inch-high raised floors for the grids of cable routes. SOM achieved a new clear height of ten feet by removing the existing mechanical systems overhead and locating new fan coil units at the building's perimeter and core. In addition to the trading floors are associated amenities: offices, video conferencing areas, copy centers, coat rooms, and food service facilities. The materials palette, sympathetic to the original structure, includes stone, stainless steel, cherry paneling, and, on core enclosures, a highly durable polyester resin finish. A spiral stair of stone and steel connects the project's three levels. Total designed area is 73,200 square feet.

Above: One of the two trading floors.
Right: Stone and steel connecting stair.
Photography: Jon Miller, Hedrich Blessing

Skidmore, Owings & Merrill LLP

Goldman, Sachs & Co.
Superbooth at New York Stock Exchange
New York, New York

The first technologically upgraded trading station completed as part of a pilot program on the floor of the New York Stock Exchange, the Goldman Sachs "superbooth" brings the technical capabilities and design quality of Goldman Sachs's own trading desk to its traders on the floor of the exchange. A modular integrated datawall at the rear of the booth centrally houses all CPUs and peripherals and provides market data information from a variety of worldwide sources including NYSE ticker quotes, four video news service providers, and a continually updated data board. This same wall provides additional cooling capacity and storage areas for the eight trading positions that flank both sides. Two-way video connections linked to multiple Goldman Sachs trading facilities allow for seamless communication, and computer workstations are equipped with the same capabilities as those at the trading desk and enable brokers to execute orders more rapidly and efficiently. Multi-line phones with speed dialing and conferencing capabilities replace old single-line models, and experimental voice-activated order processors have been implemented. Comfortable, ergonomically designed seating placed at curvilinear synthetic countertops establish a level of design quality consistent with the Goldman Sachs headquarters. The superbooth is gently lit by diffused light reflected from the suspended curved ceiling.

Skidmore, Owings & Merrill LLP

Kirkland & Ellis Law Offices
New York, New York

The planning module is a frequently employed tool for bringing order and cohesion to today's corporate interiors, but seldom has it been used more pervasively or more persuasively than in the two-floor, 48,000-square-foot Manhattan offices for the law firm of Kirkland and Ellis. The resultant order is joined by a liberating sense of openness and light, with perimeter offices largely enclosed in glass. Where privacy was wanted for lawyers' offices, a pearlescent glass layer was laminated between two ribbed layers, blocking the view but still transmitting the light.

The heart of the office is a two-story law library, featuring a dramatic stair that, with open risers and laminated glass treads, continues the theme of lightness.

Left: Reception area under a metal grid.
Right: The double-height library and its glass stair.
Photography: Michael Moran

Skidmore, Owings & Merrill LLP

Wilkahn Showroom
New York, New York

The two floors of Wilkahn North America's 6,500-square-foot showroom are not contiguous and are connected only tangentially by a striking steel stair, its upper run suspended from above on cables. Designed to dramatically showcase the company's products and furniture, Wilkahn's first showroom in New York features exposed concrete ceilings and floors as foils to the firm's precision-finished furniture manufactured in Germany. The company's logo is used as pulls on the entry doors for both floors, and together with the freestanding column painted in Wilkahn's corporate green, reinforces the showroom's identity. An inclined plane of stainless steel mesh bisects the lower floor and both directs visitors through the space and separates furniture under development from items already in the product line. Furniture is also displayed on the upper floor, which serves as the company's operations center. Office areas there can be enclosed by pivoting lacquered panels located on a diagonal axis with concrete planters on the outside terrace, creating a forced perspective within the space. The 2,500-square-foot terrace provides additional exhibition area and serves as a setting for receptions, lunches, and other gatherings.

Above and right: Highly flexible showroom space bisected by a scrim of steel mesh.
Photography: Jon Miller, Hedrich Blessing.

Spector Knapp & Baughman, Ltd.

1818 North Street, NW

Suite 510

Washington, DC 20036

202.332.2434

202.328.4547 (Fax)

Spector Knapp & Baughman, Ltd.

Xerox Document University
West Building
Leesburg, Virginia

Above: *Building exterior.*
Left: *Auditorium.*
Below: *Vaulted circulation area.*
Photography: *Ken Wyner.*

Right: *Office reception area.*
Below, right: *Auditorium reception area.*

On a secluded hill overlooking the Potomac River is the 1.1-million-square-foot campus of the Xerox Learning and Conference Center. The project shown here is a recent addition to that campus, a 140,000-square-foot multipurpose structure containing an auditorium, a document operation center, educational facilities, administrative offices, guest registration area, warehouses, and maintenance shops. These last "service areas" are camouflaged from public view, built into the side of a hill, and connected to other facilities by an underground tunnel. The entrance lobby, seen at right, features a generous ceiling height and a specially commissioned mobile of aluminum prisms. Concrete, steel, and glass are the most prominent materials in building elements roofed with copper, and lighting is unique to each space, including computer-controlled lighting effects in the auditorium. Working with this limited materials palette and with a strict proportional system, according to the designers, enabled them to achieve "a balance of plasticity in form and extreme rationality in organization."

Spector Knapp & Baughman, Ltd.

Southern Company
Washington, DC

Eight years ago, Spector, Knapp & Baughman was hired to design a very traditional office for this international electric utility company, with interiors reflecting the company's southern roots.

Recently, the company wanted the office renovated in a more contemporary spirit, and they wanted to continue working in their space throughout the renovation process. The previ-

Above: The reception area.
Left: Corridor with art work.
Photography: Andrew Lautman.

ous traditional scheme was therefore used as a departure point for the new design. Moldings and elaborate window treatments were scaled back in favor of a more streamlined scheme with contemporary accents. Some existing high-end furniture pieces were re-used, but newly added pieces were lighter in feeling, and new custom carpet designs incorporate stripes and insets to help direct the traffic flow. The new color palette is neutral with a few vibrant accents, and the new materials palette combines warm woods and cool metals. Twenty employees of the Southern Company are housed in these renovated quarters, which total 7,000 square feet.

Below: *Conference room.*
Bottom of page: *Conference room detail.*

Spector Knapp & Baughman, Ltd.

National Association
of Manufacturers
Washington, DC

Left: Reception area for the conference center.
Below: Reception desk seen from elevator lobby.
Photography: Andrew Lautman.

Above, right: Reception area detail.
Right: Credenza detail in the conference center.

The National Association of Manufacturers (NAM) is a Washington-based organization that represents thousands of manufacturers nationwide, makers of everything from widgets to drywall, from paint cans to furniture. When the entire 45,000-square-foot sixth floor of their building at 1331 Pennsylvania Avenue became available, NAM seized the opportunity to consolidate their operations and 200 employees on a single level and, at the same time, to update their image. Although the single floor promised efficiency, the extremely eccentric building shape — two narrow rectangular wings linked by an even narrower passage — presented thorny planning problems. Workstations here have been made smaller and more efficient than in NAM's previous quarters, but the amount of meeting spaces has been increased as a trade-off. The result works. As Linda Chandler, NAM's general counsel, puts it: "This space meets our functional and aesthetic goals while beautifully showcasing our members' products. It's a great solution!"

Spector Knapp & Baughman, Ltd.

Pennie & Edmonds
Law Offices
Washington, DC

Above, right:
Ceiling fixtures in the conference room.
Right: *Visitor waiting area.*
Below, right: *Reception desk as seen from entrance.*
Photography: *Ken Wyner.*

Spector, Knapp & Baughman was retained by the law firm of Pennie & Edmonds for the design of its 31,000-square-foot Washington office. A dignified image was desired, but an inviting presence was wanted as well. Wood-framed glass partitions are used throughout for a sense of openness. A large, divisible conference room was located in view of the reception area and features a lightweight, easily configurable table. File corridors with printer stations and custom storage units at secretarial areas increase filing and working space. Existing furniture was re-used and supplemented with new items in attorney offices and other high-profile areas. Sensitive to the logistical challenges of the client's relocation, the designers led the Pennie & Edmonds team in the coordination of their move-in.

Swanke Hayden Connell Architects

295 Lafayette Street
New York
New York 10012
212.226.9696
212.219.0059 (Fax)
*@shca.com

One Thomas Circle, NW
Suite 580
Washington, D.C. 20005
202.785.3331
202.785.3902 (Fax)
*@dc.shca.com

First Union Financial Center
200 South Biscayne Blvd.
Suite 970
Miami
Florida 33131-2300
305.536.8600
305.536.8610 (Fax)
*@miami.shca.com

84 West Park Place
Stamford
Connecticut 06901
203.348.9696
203.348.9914 (Fax)
*@stamford.shca.com

25 Christopher Street
London
England EC2A 2BS
44171.454.8200
44171.454.8400 (Fax)
*@london.scha.com

Mithat Ulu Unlu Sok.
No: 21, D8
Zincirlikuyu
Istanbul
Turkey 80300
90.212.212.2420
90.212.212.2328 (Fax)
gereral@istanbul.scha.com

Swanke Hayden Connell Architects

Joseph E. Seagram & Sons, Inc.
North American Shared Services Center
Delray Beach, Florida

This project for Seagram required the complete renovation of 54,000 square feet of space in an existing facility. A complicated building footprint had to be adapted from a plan devoted to private offices to one accommodating an open landscape configuration. The result needed to be orderly yet flexible. During the programming stage, therefore, a functional workstation module was developed that could be repeated throughout the installation, and during the design stage, attention was focused on well-organized circulation. Supplementing the new work spaces are some private offices, a computer center, a cafeteria for the 300 on-site employees, and a product display area. Colors are warm and bright, and, at open areas, indirect lighting brightens ceiling planes while avoiding glare at work-

Above: Seagram logo at entrance.
Right: Sitting area with conference room beyond.
Photography: Thomas Delbech.

stations. Glass pendant lighting fixtures are also used, and prominent materials include painted gypsum board, granite, carpet, and anigré wood. Swanke Hayden Connell was responsible for a full range of interior design services including graphic design.

Above: *Lounge area framed by product display.*
Right: *Workstation with indirect lighting.*

Swanke Hayden Connell Architects

IBM Corporate Headquarters
Armonk, New York

Left: Third-floor corridor connecting executive offices with boardroom and dining suite.
Below, left: Typical workstation bays.
Below, right: Executive dining corridor with walls of anigré, floors of polished granite.
Opposite: Third-floor boardroom with custom chandelier, walls of anigré and stainless steel.
Photography: Peter Paige.

This new headquarters building for the computer industry giant accommodates more than 600 employees. The space is spread over four floors that are typically very irregular in shape (being broken into three connected wings) and very large in size (85,000 square feet each). Open-plan workstations were created here, not only for clerical workers and middle management, but also for IBM's executive level. These workstations are in small clusters and have been designed with fine materials (such as anigré veneer) and meticulous attention to detail. There are also a fitness center, a cafeteria, and a conference center that offers an integration of state-of-the-art information technology, audio-visual, and teleconferencing equipment. The color palette is of earth tones and neutral greens. Materials, in addition to anigré, are fine fabrics, granite, sandblasted glass , and stainless steel with a glass bead finish. Services performed by Swanke Hayden Connell were interior design, furniture selection, custom furniture design, graphic design, and exhibition design. Total square footage was 280,000.

Swanke Hayden Connell Architects

Avon Products, Inc.
World and U.S. Headquarters
New York, New York

Avon, the international beauty products marketing corporation, moved a thousand of its employees into this 375,000-square-foot facility spread over seven floors in two neighboring Manhattan buildings. Swanke Hayden Connell's responsibilities included four key tasks: The first was to build a consensus among the Avon staff about the environment needed. This was accomplished through a series of full-scale mock-ups that were evaluated for both aesthetic appeal and performance. Second was the creation of a small number of workstation types with flexible componentry that could meet a large number of job requirements. Third was to provide some of the attributes of private offices in these open workstations. This necessitated the use of varying workstation sizes, panel heights, entry orientations, and materials. And the fourth key task was to provide extensive storage of products and supplies and access to shared technology, all within close proximity to the open work areas.

Above: *One of the workstation types.*
Below, left: *Elevator lobby.*

Some storage was actually integrated into the workstations themselves. Beyond the work areas, other headquarters facilities are a boardroom, executive office suites, conference center, cafeteria, kitchen, and servery, an employee store, a jewelry studio, and product testing laboratories. The warm, neutral color palette is accented with jewel tones, and the materials palette includes makore and anigré veneers, lacquered wood, patterned sandblasted glass, marble, silk wallcoverings, and handpainted wall finishes. Throughout the installation, the nature of Avon's business is recalled in integrated product displays.

Ted Moudis Associates

305 East 46th Street

New York

New York 10017

212.308.4000

212.644.8673 (Fax)

tma@tedmoudis.com

www.tedmoudis.com

Ted Moudis Associates

Ted Moudis Associates

Herzog Heine Geduld
Jersey City, New Jersey

The client is a 75-year-old financial services firm and a NASDAQ Market Maker. It has employed the services of Ted Moudis Associates for more than 15 years. Recently it moved its 100,000-square-foot headquarters from New York's financial district to this four-floor location in Jersey City. A staff of 500 is accommodated here, and facilities include a reception area, partners' offices, boardroom, conference rooms, and operational areas using open plan furniture systems. Most demanding was a trading floor with 200 positions, designed with attention to needs for auxiliary HVAC, for indirect lighting to reduce glare, for acoustical treatments to enhance sound carriage, and for emergency power backup. The trading desk itself was custom designed for maximum flexibility as technology develops. Similarly, the whole installation anticipates change and future personnel movement with minimal disruption of the client's operations. Towards this goal, an innovative "highway street grid" was developed to heighten the flexibility of the under-floor telecommunications network.

This page, top row, left: *Main reception room. Beyond the reception desk, glass doors lead to Boardroom.*
This page, top row, right: *Trading floor.*
Bottom of page: *President's office.*
Photography: *Elliot Fine.*

Left: *Viewing room overlooking trading floor.*
Below: *Executive boardroom.*

Ted Moudis Associates

Banpais
New York, New York

Banpais, A Mexican banking corporation, required the thorough renovation of 10,000 square feet of Manhattan office space for its day-to-day business and for its hosting of receptions. Because the facility occupies an entire floor, it was possible for Ted Moudis Associates to thoroughly design the elevator lobby with pendant lighting fixtures and geometrically pat-terned marble floor. Beyond the full-height glass entrance doors, mahogany, douka, and sapele woods share the limelight with the bank's extensive collection of Mexican art. The board-room seats 16 at a cus-tom-designed mahogany table, and an expansive executive waiting area doubles as a site for meetings, parties, and special events. Services performed at Ted Moudis Associates included programming, site evaluation and selec-tion, design, contract document preparation, and project administra-tion.

Opposite page, above: Reception area.
Opposite page, below: Executive waiting room with opening to reception area.
This page, above: Entrance lobby.
This page, below: Conference room.
Photography: Jay Rosenblatt.

341

Ted Moudis Associates

Sherwood Securities
Jersey City, New Jersey

A client since 1985, Sherwood, a financial services company needed help in their new design/move. Ted Moudis Associates designed a new 36,500-square-foot office space with a tiered trading room accommodating 180 positions with a vaulted acoustical ceiling, indirect lighting, auxiliary air conditioning, and a high level of flexibility. Included is a 3,000-square-foot voice and data equipment room with state-of-the-art equipment. Traders also enjoy a multi-function conference/meeting room with fully integrated audio-visual teleconferencing system, and an exective boardroom is similarly equipped. The data and telecommunications infrastructure employs local and wide-area networks, an unin- terrupted power system, and emergency genera- tor back-up. Throughout the office, a card access security system has been installed.

Far left: Trading room.
Left: Boardroom.
Left, below: Executive waiting area with view, through glass wall, to boardroom.
Photography: Elliot Fine.

Ted Moudis Associates

Cowles Business Media
New York, New York

Cowles Business Media is a subsidiary of a major Wisconsin newspaper. It retained Ted Moudis Associates to provide programming, site evaluation, design, construction documents, and project administration services for this 12,000-square-foot training and seminar complex for its publishers and editors. Highly sophisticated audio-visual and teleconferencing facilities were required, as was a high degree of flexibility in spatial configuration. At the heart of the installation is an 80-person main training room that can be subdivided with movable partitions into smaller areas. The room's training tables can also be easily divided or even collapsed and stored. Stacking chairs can then be brought in, and the room can serve as a small theater or lecture hall. Lighting, of course, had to be flexible as well, the solution employing a number of innovative coves, sconces, and indirect fixtures. Ted Moudis Associates successfully met both the client's 26 week schedule and its budget.

TVS Interiors, Inc.

2700 Promenade Two
1230 Peachtree Street, NE
Atlanta
Georgia 30309.3591
404.888.6600
404.888.6700 (Fax)

TVS Interiors, Inc.

The Offices of TVS & Associates
Atlanta, Georgia

Right: Cantilevered cherry stairs beside a suspended yellow ceiling plane.
Below: Reception and waiting area.
Photography: Brian Gassel/TVS & Associates.

Right: Private and semi-private work areas.
Far right: Reception room detail with Mackintosh chair design.
Below, left: Conference room with stained glass panels flanking door.
Below, right: Corridor to conference room. Wood bowl by Ed Moulthrop.

TVS & Associates' self-designed quarters for its 200-person staff occupy 66,000 square feet on the 26th through 28th floors of Atlanta's Promenade Two tower. The main entrance on the middle floor greets visitors with the dramatic overhead streak of a bright yellow ceiling plane, its angled form creating a false perspective leading to the reception area. At its opposite end, cantilevered stairs of Brazilian cherry access other floors. Throughout, such colorful drywall forms, as well as tilted panels of pearwood veneer and smaller details of charcoal-stained mahogany direct attention to key spaces and prized art. These include furniture designs by architects Charles Rennie Mackintosh and Frank Lloyd Wright, bowls carved by local artist Ed Moulthrop, and stained glass panels by Seranda Vespermann. The project garnered both national and state awards from the American Society of Interior Designers.

TVS Interiors, Inc.

Prince Street Technologies
Corporate Office/Showroom/Manufacturing Facility
Cartersville, Georgia

On a 25-acre site in Cartersville, Georgia, this facility for a major carpet manufacturer combines 170,000 square feet of manufacturing plant with 40,000 square feet devoted to office, showroom, and laboratory areas. It thus unifies a staff previously housed in three different facilities, and the new togertherness was a major design goal. One contribution to teamwork was the elimination of all enclosed offices, even for the CEO. Only two types of workstations are used in the entire installation, one eight feet by eight, the other ten by twelve. Informal conference areas, including comfortable sofas among the workstations, are liberal-

348

ly placed, and the main reception area, known as "the living room" is also used for casual employee chats. For more formal or more private meetings, there are glass-enclosed conference rooms as well. Care was taken to provide environmentally sound materials throughout.

TVS Interiors, Inc.

United Parcel Service
World Headquarters
Atlanta, Georgia

Occupying 620,000 square feet of office space and an equal amount of structured parking, this new world headquarters for UPS occupies a spectacularly wooded 36-acre site in the outskirts of Atlanta. The site is rent by a dramatic ravine with a stream cascading through it, and the building design by Thompson, Ventulett, Stainback & Associates capitalizes on the topography by bridging the crevice with a four-story bridge-like structure. Anchoring each end of the bridge are seven-story towers. Within, 1,800 UPS employees, most of them brought from UPS's former quarters in Greenwich, Connecticut, are accommodated in quarters that enjoy not only the woodland views but also an unusual complement of interior amenities: offices both open and closed, of course, but also boardroom-like conference rooms, training

Left, above: Waiting area with view of the wooded site.
Left: Conference center, auditorium.
Right: Boardroom-type conference room.
Photography: Brian Gassel/TVS & Associates.

350

rooms, an auditorium, art gallery, fitness center, audio/visual production studio, 620-seat cafeteria on two levels of the bridge structure, atrium, and roof garden. Interior colors, textures, and materials have been chosen to harmonize with the abundantly evident natural surroundings: ashlar-patterned granite, silk-paneled walls, surfaces of non-endangered mahogany, makore, and sapele woods, custom-colored carpeting. TVS&A and TVS Interiors Inc. won the commission in competition with 40 other contenders, a group narrowed to six, then finally to one.

Above, left: Connector structure open to light and view.
Top of page and above: Two views illustrating United Parcel Service's executive offices and art program for employees and visitors. The cultures of customers around the world are represented.

VOA Associates
Incorporated

224 South Michigan Avenue

Chicago

Illinois 60604

312.554.1400

312.554.1412 (Fax)

VOA Associates Incorporated

Apollo Travel Services
Rolling Meadows, Illinois

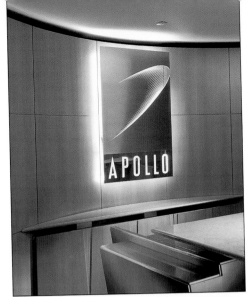

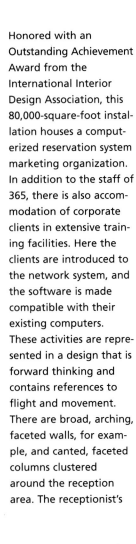

Honored with an Outstanding Achievement Award from the International Interior Design Association, this 80,000-square-foot installation houses a computerized reservation system marketing organization. In addition to the staff of 365, there is also accommodation of corporate clients in extensive training facilities. Here the clients are introduced to the network system, and the software is made compatible with their existing computers. These activities are represented in a design that is forward thinking and contains references to flight and movement. There are broad, arching, faceted walls, for example, and canted, faceted columns clustered around the reception area. The receptionist's desk is also a composition of faceted planes, and the general spatial organization is in a sweeping curve. Principal materials are pearwood, brushed stainless steel, and lacquer finishes.

Despite these impressive effects, cost for the three-floor installation was held to $27.48 per square foot.

VOA Associates Incorporated

The Attic Club
Chicago, Illinois

David Adler (1888-1949) was a distinguished Chicago architect, once an apprentice to Howard Van Doren Shaw, later a designer on his own of eclectic country houses, townhouses, and apartments for the wealthy. In 1934, on the top levels of the Field Building, Adler designed space for the Attic Club with a distinct but restrained Art Deco flavor. Buried under a number of subsequent redesigns, Adler's decor was forgotten until discovered as VOA was designing a renovation of the quarters for LaSalle National Bank, a subsidiary of the Netherlands-based ABN-AMRO Services Company.

The space is a small part of a large (700,000 square feet on 25 floors) VOA commission for ABN-AMRO. The Adler room seen here now functions again as a dining room seating 66. It has been restored in accordance with the LaSalle Bank image and also in accordance with Adler's design intentions. Some original elements, such as a single nickel-finished wall sconce, were found, restored, and used as models for new additions. The total size of the double-height room and its steel-railed mezzanine is 6,000 square feet.

VOA Associates Incorporated

Scudder, Stevens & Clark
Chicago, Illinois

These new regional headquarters for a global investment firm occupy the entire 54th floor of a Chicago tower. Happily, this particular building, chosen in a site selection process partly guided by VOA, has floors of only 14,000 square feet, the small floor plate allowing many of the office's 40 occupants to be near the glazed perimeter and its dazzling views of city, river, and lake. Once the location was fixed, VOA's duties were to develop an attractive yet functional space that was not excessively expensive. The most prominent features of the design solution are three classically-inspired rooms: a barrel-vaulted elevator lobby, a domed reception pavilion that is oval in plan, and a circular rotunda for circulation and visitor waiting. All three are impressively covered with coffered ceilings that appear to be plaster but are, in

Right: *Coffered vault over the elevator lobby.*
Photography: *Steve Hall, Hedrich Blessing.*

Left: *A cluster of open-plan work stations.*
Right: *Conference room with dramatic views.*

fact, fiberglass, a material considerably less in both weight and cost. The circular room is also graced with a custom-designed area rug. Other facilities are three large corner offices, a corner conference room, a small trading area, and a number of universally sized, custom-millwork workstations. A full-service employee lounge and kitchen also enjoys the building's views, and such equipment as files, fax machines, and printers are housed in architectural elements acting as backdrops for the workstations. As the satisfied client puts it, "VOA gave us a quietly elegant environment.... There's nothing we would do differently."

Above and on our cover: *Visitor's waiting area in the rotunda.* **Left:** *Another rotunda view.*

Ziegler Cooper

1331 Lamar

Suite 1450

Houston

Texas 77010

713.654.0000

713.654.1841 (Fax)

sziegler@zcainc.com

Ziegler Cooper

Louisiana Place
Houston, Texas

The goal of this project was nothing less than to successfully reposition a high-rise tower in the downtown Houston office market. The building was the 35-floor, 875,000-square-foot Louisiana Place, and the client was the building management firm of Jones Lang Wootton USA. Components of the repositioning were the removal of all vestiges of the building's former character and the creation of a more prominent and dynamic street presence. To these ends, the designers created new corner entrances enhanced by cantilevered canopies and eliminated parts of the building's second floor to give new height to the lobby. A structural glass curtain wall provides new transparency and depth. A rich new materials palette includes Luna Pearl granite, Absolute black granite, figured anigré wood, stainless steel, and painted metal panels. Critical to the renovation's success are new lighting treatments: accent lighting for articulated ceiling coves, ambient lighting to enhance evening views from street into lobby, and custom-designed pendant strip lighting.

Above: *New lobby area.*
Left: *View into lobby from street.*
Below: *Detail of reception desk.*
Right: *Elevator lobby on upper floor.*
Photography: *Joe Aker, Aker/Zvonkovic Photography*

Ziegler Cooper

For the T. E. Products Pipeline Company (TEPPCO), a firm dealing in oil and gas, Ziegler Cooper designed offices totalling 58,000 square feet on three floors of a Houston highrise. The installation houses 205 workers, and its design reflects the client culture by giving perimeter window space to the staff's open plan workstations. Managers therefore have interior offices. Also interior, but centrally located and highly visible, is the computer center and pipeline dispatch room that are the operation's heart. Team spaces and "thinking alcoves" encourage employee innovation. Colors are vibrant throughout, the use of lighting and glass is innovative, and other materials include metal panels, lacquered mill-work, and drywall. Flooring is of carpet and granite.

TEPPCO
Houston, Texas

Above, right: The stair connecting three levels.
Below: Typical office corridor.
Photography:
Nick Merrick © Hedrich-Blessing.

Left: *Waiting area with classic modern furniture by Eames and Noguchi.*
Below: *Stair landing on the intermediate level.*

Ziegler Cooper McKinsey & Company
Houston, Texas

For McKinsey & Company, a management consulting firm with a diverse and prestigious clientele, Ziegler Cooper has designed a number of installations. Shown here is 60,000 square feet of space in a high-rise office building in Houston's Central Business District. It accommodates 175 McKinsey employees on two and a half floors. While many of those employees seemed to be vest served by closed private offices, located along the building perimeter, the overall spatial organization is far from traditional. Clusters of "neighborhoods" support a team-based work process, with partners, analysts, and support staff grouped together according to shared work habits, rather than hierarchy.

Above: Library/work area with internal stair for McKinsey's three floors.
Right: Team work areas with movable partitions.
Photography: Joe Aker, Aker/Zvonkovic Photography.

Decentralized support functions accompany each group. Movable silk-faced panels add flexibility and, when open, make possible the creation of a "super team room." The materials palette includes cherry paneling and neutral lacquer surfaces, with bases and accents of polished black granite. Acoustic control is achieved with sound-absorbent wall and ceiling panels and with a

Right: Reception/visitor waiting area.
Below: *Videoconferencing room.*

sound masking system. Lighting is a combination of incandescent general illuminations and indirect fluorescents. Placement of McKinsey's collection of contemporary art was an important factor in the schematic design phase, and Ziegler Cooper's range of responsibilities extended to furnishings and graphic design.

Ziegler Cooper

McKinsey & Company
Dallas, Texas

Ziegler Cooper has designed 52,000 square feet for McKinsey in Dallas. Two-thirds of the space, on the 51st and 52nd floors of a downtown high-rise, was designed a dozen years ago, and the client recently returned to Ziegler Cooper for help with its expansion onto the 53rd floor. But the new space is not simply more of the same; Ziegler Cooper associate principal James E. Hanlin calls it an "experiment in new ways to work." The atmosphere is creative, the colors light and bright, the furnishings contemporary, the plan team-based and flexible. Laminated glass panels, some with rice paper inserts, help spread the light.

Right: On the newly added top floor, one of a pair of seminar areas under a soaring glass roof. A row of Eames chairs faces a "write wall."
Below, left: Informal meeting area.
Below, right: One of four private conference rooms with glass wall, communications equipment.
Photography: Joe Aker, Aker/Zvonkovic Photography.

AIA
THE AMERICAN INSTITUTE OF ARCHITECTS

Interior / Renovation of Historic Landmark; Swatt Architects.

We took all Levi Strauss & Co.'s™ figures and created a great fit.

Levi Strauss & Co. asked their architect to create a workplace as comfortable and functional as their jeans. The San Francisco Ice House renovation is tailor-made for their team-oriented philosophy and cost-effective management style. Has it worked? Since 1990, productivity, sales and profits are up. And good design played an important part. To learn how 10 other businesses profited through their architects, call 800-AIA-9930. Or point your browser at http://www.aia.org.

We make your bottom line beautiful.

Don't Let Your 9to5
Ruin Your 5to9

The single greatest cause of workplace complaints and lost productivity is chronic back pain, with billions of dollars in medical claims every year. People who sit correctly from 9 to 5 have more fun from 5 to 9. That's why everyone loves our Cyncro Ergonomic Seating, from the secretary and the computer guy, to the designer and even the CEO. Cyncro Chairs are the perfect combination of function, quality, and affordability. There are over thirty different styles of seating to choose from in our new catalogue. Call us toll-free today: 1-888-925-RUDD. We'll put you in touch with a Rudd Rep.

Rudd's Wiser.

Rudd
NO MORE BAD CHAIR DAYS

XOREL® a million double rubs

Xorel Structures   design: Anne Beetz

Xorel Chair   design: Brian Kane

(800) 727-6770

Carnegi

Geiger BRICKEL

Geiger Brickel has established itself as one of the premier seating manufacturers in North America with one of the most versatile, comprehensive, and affordable collections in the industry. Geiger Brickel seating represents classic design, quality craftsmanship, innovative details, and competitive pricing. Designers Ward Bennett, Timothy deFiebre, Anthony Garrett, and Bernd Münzebrock have created an expansive collection of guest chairs, lounge seating, and swivel chairs that not only dovetail with Geiger Brickel tables and casegoods but are suited to a variety of architectural statements. All wood chairs and lounge seating are available in a wide variety of finishes and textile choices. To learn more about Geiger Brickel and to find the Geiger Brickel sales representative or dealer nearest you, call 1.800.444.8812, or visit our website at WWW.GEIGERBRICKEL.COM.

seating collections

CLOCKWISE UPPER RIGHT: COLLEGEVILLE ARMLESS™ CHAIRS, SQUARE DEAL™ CHAIRS WITH WRITING TABLETS, COLLEGEVILLE™ CHAIRS

CLOCKWISE UPPER LEFT: ATTACHÉ™ DESK CHAIR, WOVEN™ CHAIRS, GARRETT™ LOUNGE SEATING, BRECK™ CHAIR, PINPOINT™ CHAIRS

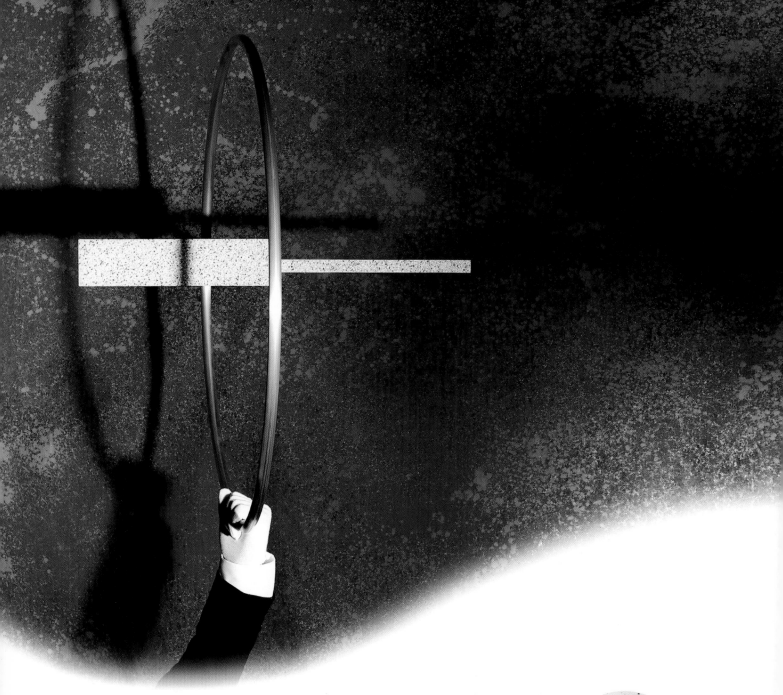

Solid surfacing made affordable.

Just say the magic words. Wilsonart® SSV™. It's a product so revolutionary, it's almost like magic. The key feature is its thickness. Not traditional 1/2-inch, but 1/8-inch. This not only drives down the cost by 25% – 45%, but it makes SSV more versatile than ever. So whether your needs range from worktops and tables to vertical panels, toilet partitions and casework, look to the one product that will transform the way you view solid surfacing. Wilsonart SSV Solid Surfacing. Incredibly durable. Renewable and repairable. Backed by a 10-year installed, transferable limited warranty. Call 1-800-433-3222 or visit our website at www.wilsonart.com.

Lauren Rottet

[solutions come from desire]

two minds. unprecedented thinking. texture. form. color. [Fundamental Logic]

Bob Hutchison

Lees

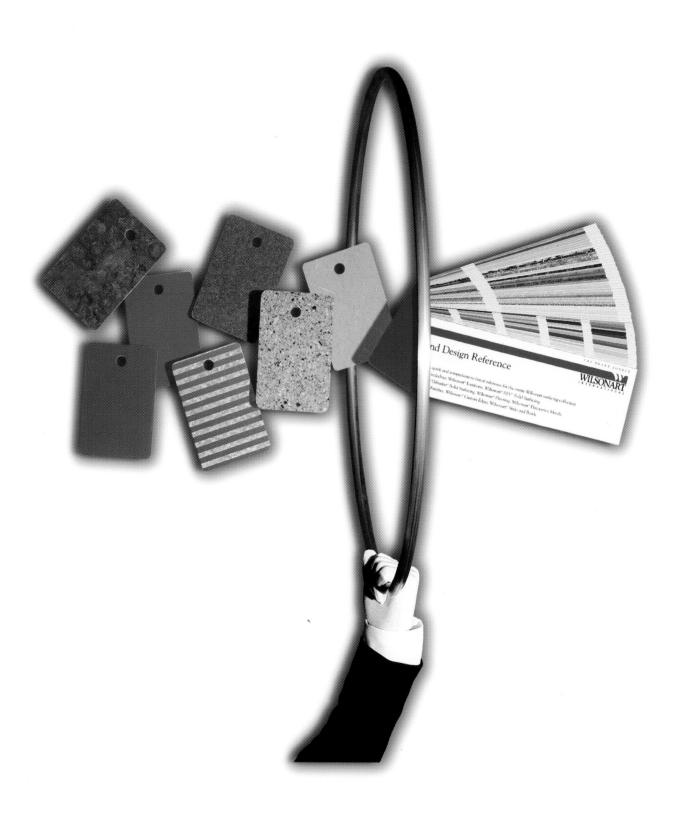

Magic Act. It's no illusion. All the updated colors and patterns of Wilsonart® Laminate, Solid Surfacing and Flooring have been vividly recreated in our new *Color and Design Reference*. It is a one stop, time-saving resource that uses the latest digital printing technology to reproduce the full line of Wilsonart products. For your own copy of this unique specification tool, call 1.800.433.3222.

THE SMART SOURCE

WILSONART
INTERNATIONAL

What will the day after tomorrow look like? However visionary we may be, the future is never what we have imagined. Teknion offers [**ability**™], mobile furniture to help people work together whatever the form of the workplace. [**ability**™] can be seamlessly integrated with systems like T|O|S and Transit to serve individual, team and corporate needs. To view the full Teknion product line contact your local Teknion representative.

www.tekus.com

Teknion

Easy Mood
designed by
Fernando Urquijo

Progetto 25
designed by
Luca Meda

Unifor, Inc.
149 Fifth Avenue
New York, NY 10010

Telephone: 212.673.3434
Facsimile: 212.673.7317
E-mail: unifor@uniforinc.com

Easy Mood
designed by
Fernando Urquijo

Progetto 25
designed by
Luca Meda

Unifor, Inc.
149 Fifth Avenue
New York, NY 10010

Telephone: 212.673.3434
Facsimile: 212.673.7317
E-mail: unifor@uniforinc.com

EGAN

The Leader in Visual Systems
...and more

Change happens. TooGo Task Furnishings address this reality. Quality mobile products for both tasks and communication. Freestanding privacy screens easily reconfigure. Flexible solutions that meet your evolving requirements.

Evolving Workplaces

New Communication Technology. Capture notes and drawings electronically. Communicate locally or via the Internet. TeamBoard's interactive projection screen turns your finger into a mouse. Simple, effective and affordable configurations.

TEAM BOARD

An Egan Company

The future is coming to you. Presentation vehicles have been designed to provide both TeamBoard demonstrations and new Egan product introductions. A valuable 30 minute learning experience.

For further information on the evolving workplace, call **1-800-263-2387** or e-mail **marketing@egan.com**
Visit our website: http://**www.teamboard.com**

Girsberger makes office chairs featuring an
extensive range of functions and ergonomic
design. And to ensure that healthy sitting is
never just a Utopian dream for anyone, we
offer our chairs at a most affordable price.
By giving our chairs a unique and enduring
appearance, we also ensure that their design
will be a fitting complement to offices in the
next millenium. If you'd like to know more,
just ask for our literature on long-lasting,
comfortable and healthy sitting.

girsberger
High Performance Seating.

Girsberger Office Seating, P.O. Box 1476, Smithfield, NC 27577-1476,
Phone (919) 934-0545, Fax (919) 934-7765. CH: Girsberger AG,
CH-4922 Bützberg. D: Girsberger GmbH, D-79342 Endingen. TR: Tuna
Girsberger, Istanbul.
Showrooms: Amsterdam, Ankara, Berlin, Chicago, Istanbul, London,
Los Angeles, New York, Paris, Salzburg, Vienna.

http://www.girsberger.com

SCIENCE FUNCTION

> "**I**ntegrating systems and freestanding furniture, Kimball's Total Best Solution transformed the City of Westminster's work environment on time and on budget. "

Robert Borders, A.I.A., Principal
Shelly DiLauro, Designer
Robert Borders & Associates
Newport Beach, California

City of Westminster, California
Interior Design Firm: Robert Borders & Associates
Architectural Firm: Dougherty & Dougherty
Photographed by Tim Schermerhorn

Not just for today.

HALLER SYSTEMS™
Modular Furniture

Clear concepts are the foundation of the efficient office. Haller Systems modular furniture offers limitless options so you can create an environment that expresses your individual personality, and your own style of work. Not just for today.

For further information please call **1-800-4 Haller** and quote the following reference No.: OF1

U. Schaerer Sons Inc.
A & D Building
150 East 58th Street
New York, NY 10155
Phone 212 371 1230
Fax   212 371 1251
www.hallersystems.com

Mobili G Inc.
San Francisco Design Center
2 Henry Adams Street #341
San Francisco, CA 94103
Phone 415 431 9900
Fax   415 431 9901
www.mobilig.com

Habitad y espacio corporativo, Homero 440, Suite 502, Polanco
11560, Mexico, D.F., Phone 01152 5 254-6047, Fax 01152 5 254-6051

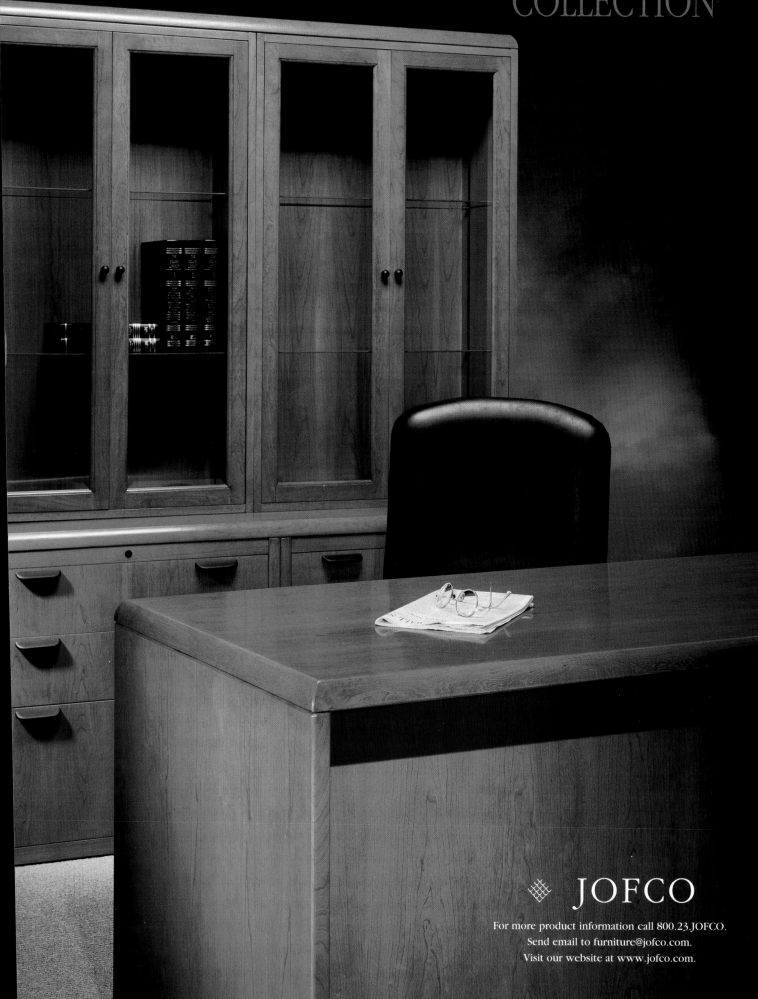

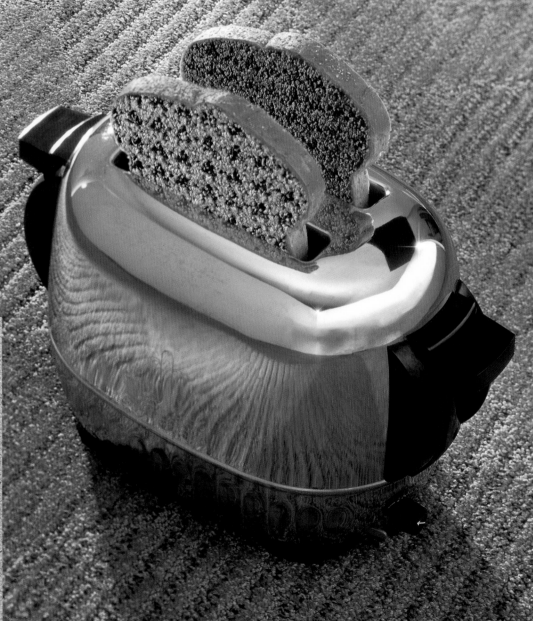

800·308·4344

Featuring Triple Density Tufting®, Constantine's patented high density tufting process

BASF *Zeftron nylon*

Pop'd Art

C

CONSTANTINE

The World's Leader in Textured Carpet.

Downlighting

High performance, unobtrusive lighting that integrates into any interior.

At Lightolier, we've spent over 90 years creating

Controls

State-of-the-art technology that provides energy savings and control over the lighting environment.

lighting that makes a difference for corporate interiors.

Track Lighting

Setting the standard for innovation, versatility and performance in accent and display lighting.

To learn more about how our wide range of fully integrated

Systems

Architecturally styled lighting that utilizes modular components to create a broad range of configurations.

products can benefit you, contact your local Lightolier

Fluorescent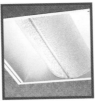

Energy efficient products employing the latest luminaire and lamp technology.

sales representative or call 800-215-1068.

Decorative

Visually distinctive, offering the perfect blend of function, style and performance.

LIGHTOLIER®

Lighting that makes a difference SM

www.lightolier.com

Mojave, from the Harbinger tufted collection of commercial carpets. 1.800.241.4216

Architectural Response Kollection, Inc

2918 Halladay Street
Santa Ana, California 92705

Tel. 714.241.7100
Fax. 714.241.7600
Toll Free 888.241.7100

Email info@ark-inc.com
Website www.ark-inc.com

Elysian's lustrous finishes
and matching woods combined
with beautiful top grain leathers
and Italian stones present
an incomparable offering of the
highest quality materials.

Architectural Response Kollection, Inc

2918 Halladay Street
Santa Ana, California 92705

Tel. 714.241.7100
Fax. 714.241.7600
Toll Free 888.241.7100

Email info@ark-inc.com
Website www.ark-inc.com

Helios is a system of freestanding,
lightly scaled office furniture
designed for the flexible needs
of the multi-functional office
environment.

What Alternative Officing (AO) Really Means

Marilyn Zelinsky

Many of the projects you've seen in this volume of Corporate Interiors use AO strategies in visible and invisible ways. For in an alternative office, the interior may *not* look much different from a traditional office, but it's the *way* in which the office is used by the employees that differs from a conventional workplace. For that reason, it takes a lot more to plan an alternative office than just reallocating space on a floorplan or in a portfolio. What it *does* take to implement a successful AO plan is the willingness to complete a greater amount of information processing than you normally would to plan and design a traditional work environment.

Quite simply put, AO is the set of strategies that companies use to meet their shifting business objectives. That set of strategies includes workspace design that supports the new ways in which people work.

This contemporary way of looking at office design began to emerge in the 1980s. When architects Philip J. Stone and Robert Luchetti wrote "Your Office Is Where You Are," an article for the March-April 1985 issue of the *Harvard Business Review,* on the alternative office (without even mentioning the term once-it hadn't yet been coined by HOK), the authors referred to the new workplace as a series of "activity settings." The authors explained that activity settings was a term describing an environment designed with a series of multiple workspaces.

Initially, people thought that AO was a single strategy of handing employees a laptop and telling them they no longer had an office in which to work. Today, most of us realize that the new workplace comprises a much broader array of solutions. Some of these spatial workplace strategies and flexible arrangements work hand-in-hand. For example, you can telecommute and hotel at the same time if your company has asked that you give up your dedicated space on the basis that you work at home more than in the office. You can telecommute and share an office. You can telecommute from a telecenter (which is like a wired-up branch office).

Keep in mind that there is a broad range of interpretations and understandings that people have of an alternative workplace solution. For example, to some clients, an alternative workplace may be defined simply as this: "AO means I will have a conferencing area in my office." Some employees aren't familiar with the terminology: "Hoteling means I get to sleep at the office," is a real comment from an anonymous employee of a large telecommunications company. Others are cynical about the whole thing: "Hoteling is a system by which cubicles are assigned to the employees as they show up each day. Nobody gets a permanent work space, and therefore no unproductive homey feelings develop," says Scott Adams, author of *The Dilbert Principal.*

GIVING THANKS TO AO PIONEERS

Even before the words "AO" were coined in the early 1990s, there was a handful of companies that took risks with their employees and stockholders to carve out unorthodox work settings that left many observers scratching their heads and gave others the inspiration to do the same thing with their own organizations. These pioneers went on the assumption that new work processes could salvage poor customer relations, foster internal communication, and reduce bloated real estate portfolios.

Who are these pioneers? No doubt one of the first experiments in AO happened back in the early 1980s when Digital Equipment Corporation in Finland took a first stab at a new kind of work environment. The main idea in this experimental office was that the office was supposed to look and feel more like a home, giving the employees a more comfortable place in which to work. The employees selected the furniture, which included recliners, and put computers on mobile tables that could be moved around within a fixed zone.

The Digital experiments paved the path for other AO projects. Take for instance the Xerox Parc Collaborative Laboratory, designed by the San Francisco-based

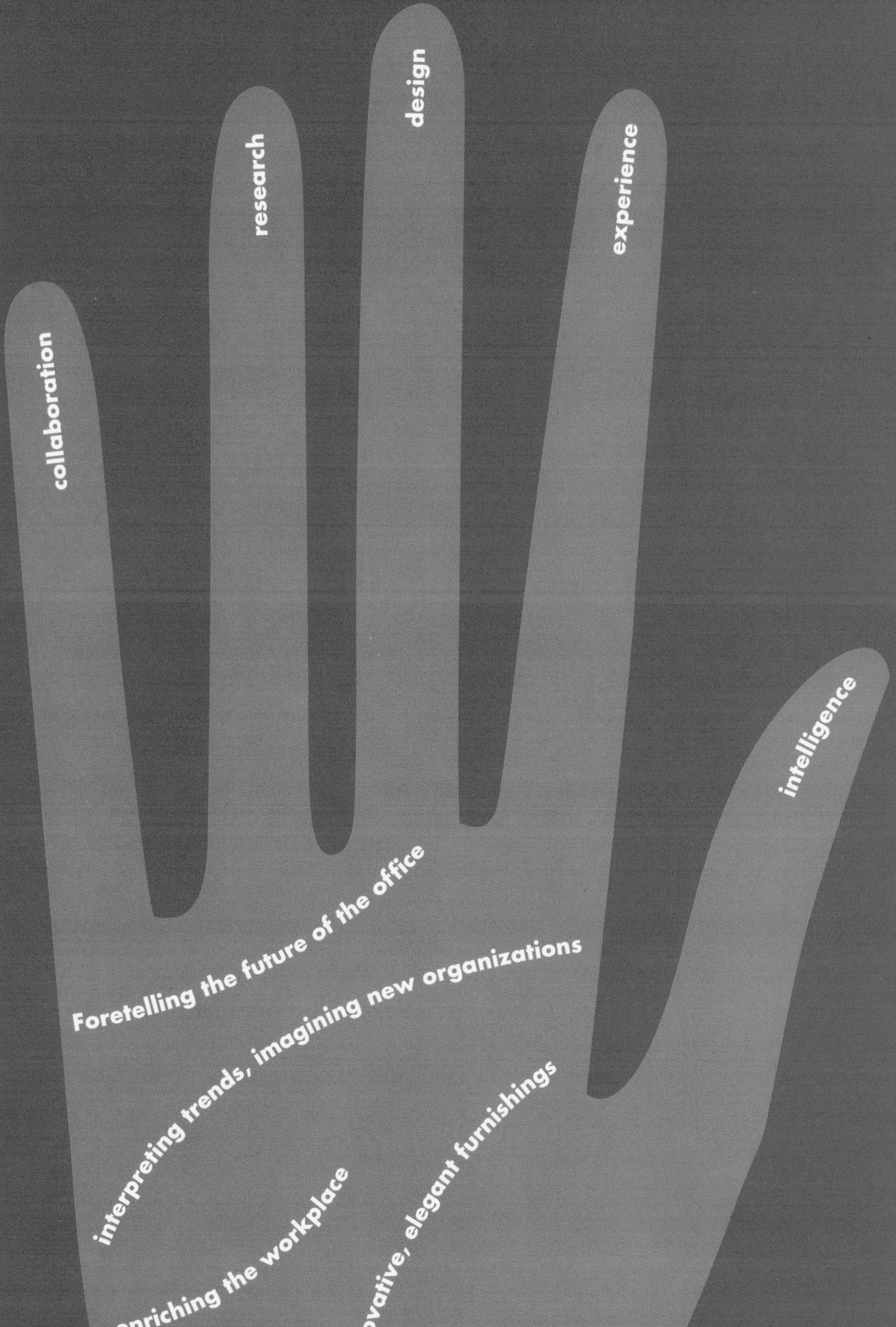
collaboration
research
design
experience
intelligence
Foretelling the future of the office
interpreting trends, imagining new organizations
enriching the workplace
with innovative, elegant furnishings

Osburn Design firm in the later 1980s. The project's objective was pure and simple: Create an environment to simplify product design and in-house communication. The one stringent design criterion given to the Osburn Design firm was to avoid using any mahogany or other luxury materials and to focus on flexibility of space and furniture. The result was a teaming environment that engaged the use of whiteboards, new patterns of thinking, new patterns of speech both internally and externally, and new ways of collaborating. Steve Osburn of Osburn Design reported: "What we were doing in 1983 for Xerox PARC was a precursor for what was to come. It was way beyond what we as an industry were doing in office design elsewhere. It was all very inspirational."

In the late 1980s and early 1990s, the floodgates were open for AO experimentation to begin its mainstream course into corporate America. In the 1980s, Andersen Consulting, a fast-growing, image-conscious management consulting firm, changed its course of building trophy facilities to reflect the changing nature of their consultants' work styles. Though consultants were demanding larger offices, the reality was that they were never in their offices.

So Andersen developed the just-in-time (JIT) office concept of officing. JIT, a term modeled on JIT manufacturing, in which inventories are kept low and parts arrive only when needed so that there is no chance of wasted materials, translated well into Andersen. The JIT office is an inventory of workspaces that accommodate an employee on an as-need basis so that there is no chance of wasted space. The JIT office began as a trial run in Andersen's San Francisco office in 1987, and the company never looked back at traditional offices again as its AO concept evolved through the years.

Following in Andersen's footsteps were Ernst & Young, KPMG Peat Marwick, Chiat/Day (now known as TBWA/Chiat/Day), IBM, American Express, AT&T,

Amdahl, and hundreds of other companies large and small, each with a unique vision of the alternative office. And though all these companies have realized the benefits of AO, they have also no doubt learned, as all new experiences and concepts teach, the traps and demands that the new workplace can place upon a company and its employees.

WHAT AO CAN AND CAN'T DO FOR YOUR COMPANY

The problem with AO is that too many CEOs and executive managers hear about AO and expect great things from it, and they expect immediate and perfect results. Most everyone is enamored with the fact that AO can potentially save millions of dollars a year on real estate portfolios, a fact that all too often drives a company's decision to dive into any or all the aforementioned strategies without forethought or planning.

"Alternative officing is not a quick fix," says John Lijewski, principal of Perkins & Will New York. "If you look at it as a sole means to real estate savings, that's a big mistake. Although the savings in real estate may be substantial, if that's driving your decision to go into alternative officing, that will severely compromise its effectiveness. Alternative officing is not a bricks and mortar solution. Alternative officing modifies human behavior because we are dealing with people."

What Lijewski says is that AO is a business-driven strategy that is used as a tool to help you achieve your business objectives. No longer is the office just a product, it's being used as part of the process of achieving a business objective. AO then becomes a strategy that becomes integrated with your company's business objectives. However, finding those objectives (and they should go deeper than real estate savings) in order for AO to succeed as a strategic business tool will help you to avoid the pitfalls of misapplied AO.

ARCHETYPE

The Archetype Table Lamp
designed by Michael Vanderbyl

Handsome styling to
discreetly complement a
myriad of design solutions.

White crepe shades offered in
round or square in two sizes each.

Metal finishes offered in
Polished Nickel, Polished
Brass or Satin Nickel.

Round or square finely
machined base with bolt
down option.

HOW TO AVOID AO PITFALLS

What are the four keys to avoiding the deep pitfalls of AO? Companies with *unsuccessful* AO programs <u>failed</u> to do the following:

- establish exactly why and for what core business goals (above and beyond reducing real estate) the company needed AO strategies.
- establish a cohesive cross-functional team at the very beginning of the project.
- learn how to sell the concept to upper management so it continues to support the effort.
- establish a change management program (including critical in-house communications programs and training programs) to help the corporate culture adjust to new work styles and norms.

Now we will explore each of these four points in more depth.

Point #1: Establishing what core business goals AO strategies will help to accomplish.

Linda Russell, senior partner in Telecommuting Consultant International, a strategic consultant firm in Canada focusing on measuring impacts of workplace options, points to this very issue. Russell maintains that the health of an AO project often falters after the program is implemented. During a teleconference in 1997 sponsored by the Telecommuting Advisory Council, Russell talked about one of her company's clients, a large oil and gas company with retail clients.

"Successful programs demonstrate three characteristics. Companies understand how they work and how working differently can affect their core business. They found ways to isolate, nurture and sustain these productivity increments over long-term. They also found ways to direct these productivity increments against critical core business tasks," says Russell. In a nutshell, she says that many companies that install AO programs fail to realize that all the productivity gains are going towards the wrong core business goals. In that case, the value of productivity gains becomes a wasted effort.

Russell tracked her client, a company that had a majority of its field sales people working from home offices with access to touch down local regional offices.

At first, the program seemed healthy and mature. The company managed to save significant real estate costs by AO. There was significant reduction in absenteeism, employees were grateful that they didn't have to commute, and there was statistically significant data indicating that employees were enjoying incremental productivity.

But when Russell began digging deeper, looking at time-use data, she realized there was trouble in paradise. It seemed only one in three workers was spending more than 25 percent of the available work time on direct customer interface. For field sales people, this was a startling finding. It was Russell's first clue that, although there was proof of incremental productivity, it was not being directed against core business issues like customer interface or customer tasks.

Where were the incremental productivity findings? Russell uncovered the fact that the workers were spending as much time in their cars filling out expense statements as they were spending on customer interface. "Hard-earned incremental productivity-won at the cost of over $15,000 per telecommuter—was being directed against a wide range of non-critical tasks. We have solid proof that this incremental productivity was flying out the window," says Russell.

There was more bad news. Both telecommuters and managers were reporting that well over 80% of the telecommuters were delivering more than satisfactory performance. That meant current definitions of performance embraced the wrong issues. In essence, the company was saying that the time spent driving in a car or filling out expense

DAVIS

COSMO COLLECTION

Interesting solutions for the single office as well as the
team work space. Freestanding elements are mobile and
can be grouped according to the functional needs.

Unmistakable looks created with
harmonious use of exciting materials
including beech, painted ash, ribbed
aluminum laminate, tinted translucent glass,
and chrome or black framework.

Designed by Wolfgang C.R. Mezger.
Licensed from Wilhelm Renz GmbH&Co.
Winner of 1997 APEX Award from IIDA.

Also shown: Webb Chair Series™

Davis Furniture Industries, Inc.

PO Box 2065, High Point, NC 27261-2065
TEL 336 889 2009
FAX 336 889 0031
E-Mail
mail@davis-furniture.com
Web Site
www.davis-furniture.com

reports was as important as time spent with customers.

So here was a company that was reaping all the expected and obvious benefits that remote work promises, but the benefits weren't being put to good use. Russell says the lesson other companies should learn from this client is that saving money through AO programs doesn't mean it's working. Saving space doesn't mean it's working. Even solid signs of incremental productivity or job satisfaction don't mean it's working.

The bottom line is this: If the incremental productivity is not being directed towards your core business challenges and directly benefiting your customer, it's not working. Companies shouldn't take the time and expense of implementing an AO strategy with the vague hope that there will be results in one form or another. You need to take the time to decide where you want to go. After you get there, you have to make a reality check to make sure that where you are is really where your company needs, and wants, to be.

Point #2: Establish a cohesive cross-functional team at the very beginning of the project.

The last thing you want to do is go at this alone. If you have initiated—or have been handed the charge to implement—AO strategies, you need to gather a group of helpful people from all walks of the company.

Gathering this group is more easily said than done because, historically, most corporations are heavily departmentalized, and each department stays within its boundaries, keeping to itself, working in a vacuum, and operating with the notion that nothing it does relates to anything initiated by the department down the hall, anyway.

The taboo of interdepartmental mingling lifted slightly in the mid-1990s as companies became frighteningly aware that departments needed to come together in order to implement projects

faster, cheaper, smarter and with more innovation than ever before. Today, disciplines from engineering to architecture to Corporate Real Estate (CRE) to Human Resources (HR) are coming together more quickly to form cross-functional teams.

Who belongs in this cross-functional team? It takes a representative from each of the following departments to grease the wheel of an AO project:

- Executive management
- HR and Training
- Technology
- Facilities
- Legal
- Financial

Note that you should always bring in a consultant with experience steeped in AO projects to augment and analyze the in-house team's efforts. Consultants will also make sure no one in-house drops the ball on the project.

What might happen, for instance, is that CRE and the collaborating design firm you've chosen to implement the AO project will begin to partner with in-house departments and develop a cross-functional team or task force that will carry along a pilot program and, ultimately, the rest of the program when it rolls out company-wide.

Point #3: Selling the idea to upper management.

Andrew Laing from DEGW Architects and Consultants makes this point about AO: "We've learned that AO is not alternative any more. No longer the prerogative of eccentric high-tech 'road warriors' or publicity-seeking creative firms, AO is becoming normal for major corporate organizations in one form or another."

Laing's point is well taken, which should take the pressure off you, the end-user. No longer should you feel that you're trying to implement some kind of crazy scheme for your organization. You don't have to feel as if you are trying to push a rock up a mountain when you are trying to sell these

Calfskin. The very best. We make it.

EDELMAN LEATHER

For leather specialist in your area call 800-886-TEDY

programs to upper management, or to your employees.

However, it could be that AO is not at the top of your CEO's list to discuss. If you ask your CEO if he or she thinks that an AO strategy would help the company be more profitable, the answer is likely to be "no." But what will get the executive management team's attention is that if the company realizes its mandate is to grow its productivity and revenue, AO is one tool to get the company to its objective by piggybacking onto a reengineering effort. Ultimately once you get the senior managements' attention, they will quickly want to know what other companies in your field are doing in the way of AO. Facility professionals will have to prove the case for AO with benchmarking other comparable companies' experiences.

Choose your benchmarks carefully. When dealing with senior management, choose your case studies so that they are relevant to your industry. Senior managers don't want to hear theoretical similarities, they want to see hard-core facts about how the competition is benefiting from AO.

The importance of finding a champion

Members of executive management may get excited over the benefits of AO, but they often demonstrate the NIMBY (not in my back yard) syndrome. Perhaps they are gung-ho at the beginning of a project because they believe that employees should work in open or universal plans, telecommute, or hotel. But when they are asked to give up their own private offices, or even shrink it down, most senior management will balk.

This is where your AO project can get into trouble, and it could sink fast unless you find an executive manager or CEO who is an ally to the AO project. Finding an executive can be difficult, but it can be done, and it is necessary because employees will resent executives who don't walk their talk.

One executive helping the AO cause is James Hackett, CEO of Steelcase. Since building its famous Leadership Community in Grand Rapids, MI, Hackett has escorted a stream of CEOs through the caves and commons executive work area where Hackett himself sits in an alternative work setting that includes Personal Harbors and teaming spaces.

"Usually CEOs are embarrassed when they see where I work, and there is a tendency toward reductiveness... They say, 'Jim, you know, my office isn't as big as you think,' and I tell them not to apologize for it because it's the way business was organized in America for a long time," says Hackett.

Point #4: Learn about your corporate culture then establish a change management program.

Frederick Taylor, inventor of Work Study and Scientific Management, called people-workers-"units of production." He preached his belief that these units of production should be organized in their workspaces for maximum efficiency. What Taylor neglected to understand, however, is that these "units of production have feelings, thoughts, ideas, beliefs, and emotions that can come together to form a web within a company of nonverbal cues called a "corporate culture."

There isn't one definition of corporate culture, but it really means the layers of unspoken cultures hidden behind departments, staffs, and relationships between colleagues and managers. You also can't assume that the corporate culture in three companies in the same industry are the same.

If you are planning an AO workplace for your company, you will be changing and dismantling a corporate culture that has been carefully built over time. Understand your company's culture before tampering with its physical setting, or you will be sorry. If you fail to do so, you will dismantle a corporate culture, destroying with it the upward curve of productivity resulting in a group of people who are now disoriented, disloyal, and who could care less about the newness or beauty of

the physical environment, much less the failures or successes of the company.

What's called for is a change management program that is three-pronged, involving the following components:

- finding a way to let employees air their concerns and grievances over an AO project
- implementing a consistent corporate communications program
- beginning consistent training programs teaching employees how to use new work space, how to use new technology, and how managers and employees can communicate with each other if one party works off-site.

Change management programs are a critical part of any AO program. They aren't new, but often they aren't executed very well or very consistently. The scenario is a common one: Company leaders talk with employees about their visions for reengineering, managers scurry to benchmark and draft up follow-up plans for process improvements, and, finally, subordinates are expected to carry out orders on those plans with unwavering support. Results often fall short, and employees usually begin to feel as if these strategies for change are merely whims issuing from the executive suite, a "flavor of the month" strategy that the CEO must have read about in the latest business magazine. The alternative workplace is susceptible to this backlash if change management efforts are handled improperly.

"An alternative workplace implementation feels like an earthquake to the employee," says Laura Compabasso, a management consultant with Progressive Strategies in Los Angeles. "It shifts the ground underneath you; it changes everything you thought about the way you work."

Consultants like Compabasso help employees ease their way into the alternative workplace. She guides managers and employees to understand the little details that will help an AO project work smoothly, such as getting procedures down pat for booking conference rooms and making sure everyone knows how to find privacy in an AO. Compabasso says that managers fail to see that everyone has different needs in the workplace and that forcing an employee to comply with an AO plan without any guidance will backfire.

But just how easy is it for a company to make a transition from traditional into an alternative workplace? The more established a company is, the easier it is to change it into an AO. More often we think it to be that a new, younger company will make the transition into AO better. But a traditional company is already established in its culture and pace, while a new company has a harder time working itself into an AO. Typically, a young company is just feeling its way around, and employees are coming together from all different backgrounds after working in a variety of different types of offices. There's a lot of uncertainty in a young company's corporate culture. So the onset of AO in the early stages of such a company can be detrimental to its stability. Before the introduction of AO, a company needs time to learn to understand its business, its product, the management style, and its coworkers.

Letting employees speak their minds:

For a young or an established company, step number one in an AO program implementation is to let the employees in on what's going on and ask for their feedback. Too many companies keep employees in the dark, especially when it comes to something like the downsizing of office space. This attitude can cause serious problems with employee morale.

Compabasso remembers one particular client who handled the AO move rather poorly, bringing people in at the last minute on the decision to move them out of private offices and into open plans. Employees felt betrayed, baffled, and wounded, says Compabasso. The lesson here is that open, direct, and constant communication is vital to employee buy-in for an AO.

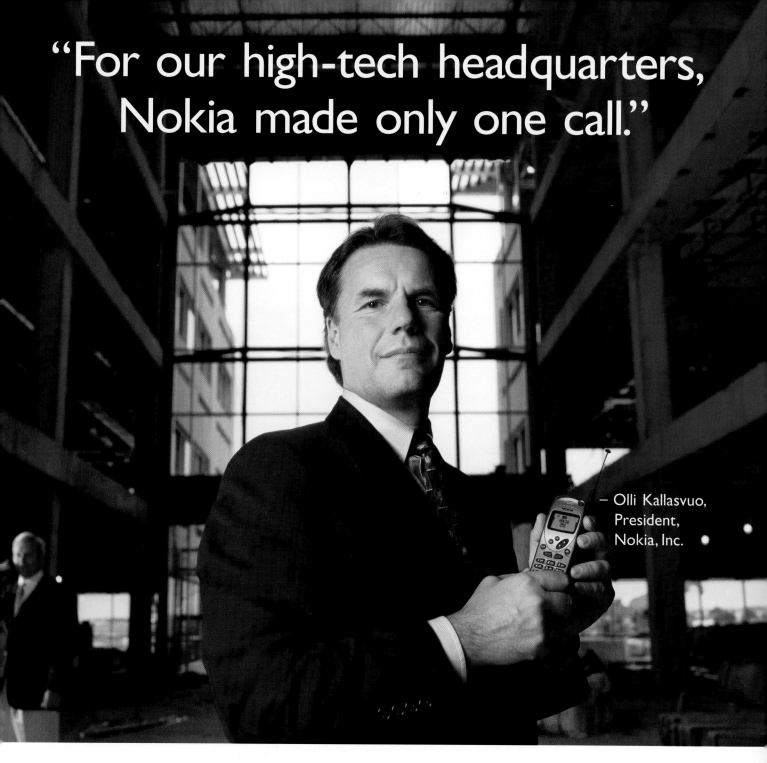

"For our high-tech headquarters, Nokia made only one call."

— Olli Kallasvuo,
President,
Nokia, Inc.

As the world's leading manufacturer of digital mobile phones and a pioneer in telecommunications technology, Nokia thrives on innovation. So when a state-of-the-art office complex was needed to establish Nokia's Americas headquarters, they knew who to call. Cushman & Wakefield.

Nokia wanted the one real estate services firm that not only understood their high-tech business, but could handle site-selection, negotiate an economic incentives package and provide ongoing construction management, now and in the future.

From our global reach to our depth of services, from our proprietary research to our creative problem-solving, we're unmatched in the industry. In fact, nobody helps more businesses of all sizes, here and around the world.

To find out how we can help you, give us a call at 1-800-346-6789.

Improving your place in the world.℠

Marina van Overbeek, workplace strategist for Cisco, a global manufacturer of computer networking equipment, had the right idea when she was implementing an AO in the company's New York office. The New York location was chosen to convert to a hoteling environment because of the division's explosive growth. Van Overbeek spoke to the entire staff population at the bottom floor of the project, showing them slides, and educating them about AO. After the presentation, the staff began what van Overbeek describes as three hours of emotional torture. "They screamed and yelled at me. I thought they were going to kill me," she remembers.

At one point she told them she wouldn't force AO down their throats, but could they work together to come up with a compromise, working together as a team to develop the office space. Van Overbeek requested that the management team in the office pull together a team of the most boisterous staffers with a few AO supporters in the group. She had the foresight to realize that, by listening to the loudest protesters, she could work on their concerns and make them feel as if someone were listening to them. The project could then be even more successful.

"The biggest lesson I learned is the importance of putting the most critical employees together on a team," van Overbeek advises. "If you don't get them involved creatively, they will get involved in a negative way." Thanks to van Overbeek's tenacity, the New York office is indeed a hoteling environment.

Yet another way of educating employees and getting their feedback at the same time is through visual education. Building a physical mock-up of what an AO environment could look and feel like gives employees the opportunity to see that it's not as foreign a concept to work in as they thought it might be. That's what Lynne Kelley-Lewicki, director of integrated workplace strategies at Cigna, the giant insurance and financial strategies company, did on the campus located outside Hartford. Lewicki built a mock-up of an activity setting to give employees the chance to learn more about the workplace of the future. She has since taken dozens of managers through the warehouse space. The tours have helped people to visualize the solution to a department-specific design issues even if they haven't resulted in all-out alternative workplace solutions.

That's the same kind of thinking Pfizer, the giant pharmaceuticals company, had when remodeling its New York headquarters into a universal floor plan designed by the New York-based design firm, Brennan Beer Gorman Monk. To get employee input on how the space could best be designed, William Whistler of Brennan Beer Gorman Monk distributed a questionnaire to everyone in the International Pharmaceuticals Group, the division to be affected by the redesign. Though Whistler says it's atypical to send out a questionnaire like that to everyone involved in the space reconfiguration project, it nonetheless signaled to the employees that this was to be a different kind of project in which management was sincerely interested in obtaining their input. As a result, the design team built mock-ups of the office and the workstations that were to be built, and then had the employees offer their comments about the prototypes. Everyone voted on the color scheme of the workspace, the glass selection, and the furniture specifications. Votes were tallied, and the results were published in an ongoing newsletter that was distributed throughout the company every six weeks.

Gunlocke

AFIFIIFI   RVP   54857   AD BJHB

s e r r a

The Gunlocke Company a HON INDUSTRIES company, One Gunlocke Drive, Wayland, NY 14572 | 800.828.6300 | Fax 716.728.8353 | http: www.gunlocke.com

design: paul james | mehmet ergelen

SAMPLE QUESTIONNAIRE

Here is a sample of the questionnaire, which differs from the one given to managers.

RESPONSIBILITIES:

1. Briefly describe your job and how you interact with others in your department or division. Describe predictable work peaks, if any, and indicate when they occur.

PERSONAL WORK AREA:

2. The following conditions affect you when you are trying to do your job. If a condition is distracting, state the amount of time you are interrupted by it each day:

- people passing by your work area

_____
Time

- awareness of other people's activities and conversations

_____
Time

- noise from office machines, telephones

_____
Time

- time it takes to get to other departments,

_____
Time

- equipment, machines, and services

_____
Time

- other

_____
Time

3. Please circle the work station you currently occupy. Note positive and negative aspects of your office, i.e. task lighting is not bright enough/too bright, guest chairs are often/ seldom used, there is sufficient/insufficient filing space, etc. (Note: line drawings of five standard furniture and office/open plan layouts were featured for employees' comments.)

4. Please indicate your overall impression of your work area by circling one number of each pair of adjectives.

attractive	1 2 3 4	unattractive
comfortable	1 2 3 4	uncomfortable
private	1 2 3 4	not private
isolated	1 2 3 4	crowded
good light	1 2 3 4	poor lighting
quiet	1 2 3 4	noisy
enough storage	1 2 3 4	not enough storage
enough work surface areas	1 2 3 4	not enough work surface areas
comfortable chair	1 2 3 4	uncomfortable chair
supports work	1 2 3 4	doesn't support work
good ventilation	1 2 3 4	poor ventilation
temperature/ comfortable	1 2 3 4	temperature/ uncomfortable

ADJACENCY REQUIREMENTS:

Please list people and groups with whom you work. Indicate the importance and basis of being adjacent to these people in your new office.

Personnel/ Team	Adjacency			Basis		
	essential	important	useful	face-to-face	exchange	team

SUPPORT AREAS:

Please indicate the support areas that you use to support your job function.

1. Duplicating and photocopying area
   ____times per day
   ____typical page total copied per usage
   ____do you utilize biding, collating, etc.?

2. Shared printers and fax machines
   ____times per day
   ____typical page total per usage

3. Shared areas
   ____Do you now, or in the future will you benefit from any shared facilities or areas not listed under any previous question? Please describe, and note that shared facilities are items such as work tables, libraries, P.C. stations, storage, supply rooms, and/or work rooms. Also note any sharing of a special piece of equipment such as a color copier, color laser printer, marker board, TV/VCR, etc.

FREE ASSOCIATION
freedom of choice + liberty to express

(800) 633-0468
breakaway, fissure, bombay, strata

Masland
contract

uncommon expression

FLOW DIAGRAM

Using the illustration as an example, please sketch the relationships between you and the people with whom you interact most frequently or who are most critical to your job function.

Legend

```
------- intermittent work flow
_____ moderate work flow
======= heavy work flow
```

Sample:

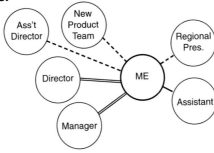

ADDITIONAL COMMENTS

Please make any other comments, suggestions, and/or recommendations regarding the work environment you wish to be considered for the new office environment. Attach additional sheets if necessary.

CORPORATE COMMUNICATIONS AND TRAINING PROGRAMS FOR AO:

Corporate communications programs are nothing new. Just about every company has an employee newsletter, a web site or Intranet, or a monthly hard paper memo service. There are plenty of ways to communicate the increments of progress of a conversion to AO so that all employees are kept up to date.

One company that is serious about its corporate communications program is Southern California Edison, the Rosemead, CA-based energy company, Southern California Edison. Brenda Laffin, head of AO, says that the best way to handle corporate communications is through newsletters and notices that are to the point and simple.

"Most of our training and presentations on AO are done with low-budget color prints or power point," she says. Laffin says there are always so many adjustments to an AO program that it makes no sense to publish anything in a final form.

What most companies fail to do is train their managers and employees on the subtle and not-so-subtle changes that AO will bring to their work processes. The worst thing you can do is to throw laptops with new software at employees, tell them to work at home or in a hoteling environment, and expect everything to work out smoothly.

"The most consistent theme found in the initial research for implementing a mobile workforce is that projects fail or succeed in proportion to the amount of mandatory user education," says John F. Frank, business leader for IBM's Workforce Mobility unit, writing about the process in an article in the *Total Quality Review* in 1995.

Every company experienced in AO has its own way to train employees for all types of AO strategies. For example, years ago at New York-based American Express, the giant credit card and financial services company, employees who volunteered to telecommute were asked to learn how to put back together a computer and printer that were literally smashed to pieces on the floor. It was American Express's way of empowering employees to troubleshoot their own computer problems when they were working from home.

More recently, New York-based financial services company Merrill Lynch instituted a new program to train telecommuters before they go home to work. The company has built a lab to help employees simulate what it would be like to work at home as a telecommuter. The lab is located on a floor within Merrill Lynch's New York facility, and anyone who volunteers to telecommute must go through a few days of working in this lab to learn what it will be like to feel work on their own and not under the watchful eye of a manager.

T I B E T A N

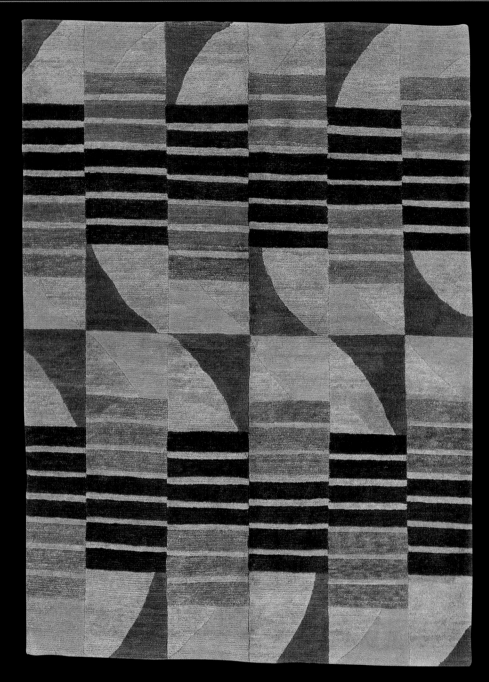

C A R P E T S

PROGRAMMED AND MADE TO ORDER DESIGNS AND SIZES.

MICHAELIAN & KOHLBERG

578 Broadway, 2nd floor New York NY, 10012   212-431-9009

THE PREMIER TRADE RESOURCE FOR DECORATIVE RUGS

But training must encompass more than just training for equipment and technology troubleshooting. In any AO scenario, whether it's hoteling, telecommuting, or universal plan, managers and employees will need to be retrained on how to communicate with one another.

AT&T's School of Business, located in Somerset, NJ, has developed a program especially for those needs. The AT&T Virtual Workplace Educational Series was designed to help business leaders, project teams, managers, and employees to better understand the issues, opportunities, and challenges associated with the alternative workplace.

The series is layered in three tiers. The first tier explores the concept of the virtual workplace, including telecommuting. The second tier trains participants about the design and implementation of an AO. The third tier gives managers and employees the opportunity to explore how they will communicate and work together differently in an AO environment so they can effectively manage necessary changes in work processes.

Once you've gathered your cross-functional team, have the blessing from executive management to continue the AO project, and have developed a change management program, now then you can get on with the design of the actual physical environment.

HOW TO WORK WITH A DESIGN FIRM ON AN AO PROJECT

There are a couple of suggestions about planning, designing, implementing, and managing an alternative office that must be considered.

First, don't panic. You won't necessarily have to trash millions of dollars of inventoried panel systems in order to have a more flexible working environment.

Second, realize that you and your cross-functional team don't have to go at this alone. If you do, it might turn into a case where the blind are leading the blind. Hire an AO expert. This, of course, can be an interior designer(s) or a strategic facility planner that has experience with AO environments. Many such experts have contributed to the projects shown in *Corporate Interiors Volume 2.*

For one thing, the roles of both the end user and the designer have changed in light of AO. Since the term facility management came into existence around 1979, it's been considered to be a service providing department. But today, no longer is a facility professional solely relegated to adjusting the temperature in someone's office. Today's FMs are professionals with backgrounds in engineering, architecture, design, finance, purchasing, or administration. FMs have been able to become more closely aligned with senior management than ever before in order to find ways to streamline facility costs.

It's still not a perfect scenario. For, even though FMs have increased their professional recognition and have become more visible as decision makers that effect a company's bottom line and aid in its core business objectives, both the FM and CRE professional still struggle to handle the downsizing of their staffs and departments while executive management continues to charge them with more responsibility.

That's where the help of a progressive strategic design firm can come in. Design firms that look at AO strategies as opportunity for new business and as a chance to learn more about their clients have created divisions to address and support client needs in this area.

Most of you say you need a designer who speaks business, who can become part of the business team that is making the decisions. You want a designer who can analyze your business, and who has the vision to help you and your company get into the future as the company's objectives evolve. A handful of design firm executives are hiring management consultants and

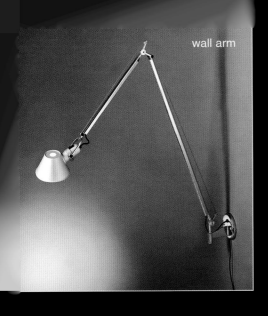
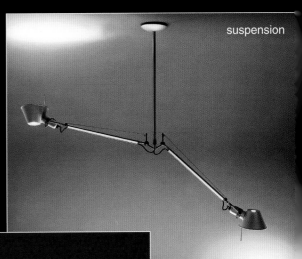

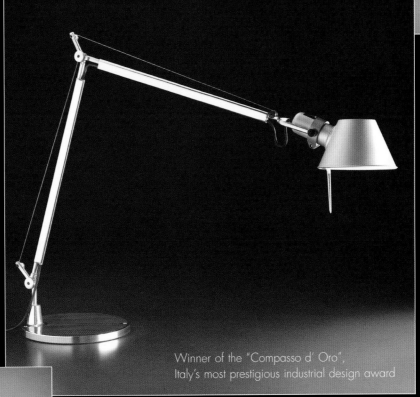
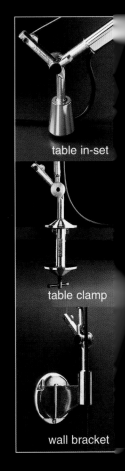
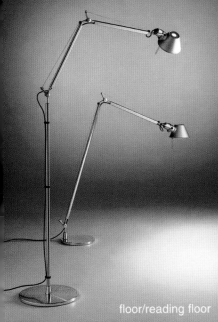

putting them into staff positions in order to help their firms speak the same language as their clients in presenting new space strategies relating to business objectives.

A FINAL THOUGHT ON "ALTERNATIVE OFFICING" FURNITURE

As was mentioned above, you don't have to get rid of millions of dollars of panel systems in order to implement a successful AO product. In fact, most manufacturers realize the importance of helping you find a way to make your panel systems more flexible to accommodate today's workstyles.

But, a few years ago, aside from Haworth's Crossings and Steelcase's Personal Harbor, it was nearly impossible to find any furniture that could support an AO project. Just ask the folks at MCI Boston Rally Center. The Boston-based firm, Hoyle, Doran & Berry Architects (HDB), the designers of the MCI Boston Rally Center, had been given the charge of designing a virtual, or hoteling, environment for the telecommunications company in 1996. The space called for a number of areas that furniture manufacturers had not yet considered. "We tried to stress to furniture manufacturers how important this project would be, but no one wanted to be flexible enough in giving MCI what we truly needed to support work. We had to rely on custom furniture," says Diane Jarry, MCI Boston Rally Center's facilities manager.

HDB needed storage lockers for virtual workers, mobile baskets for transfering files, privacy screens, and mobile tables. Screens and tables weren't difficult to find, but the lockers and baskets were. HDB vice president Ethan Anthony designed the hoteling locker unit, and Egan Visual agreed to build it. It was an item that became a line product for the manufacturer.

Another smaller company, O+O Software in Naperville, IL, experienced the same kind of frustration when it came to finding the right product for its deskless office in 1996 (featured in *Corporate Interiors,* Volume I). Naperville-based O'Neil Designers, Inc. (ODI) helped O+O find the right furniture solution, but it took two years to do it. "People thought software programmers wanted cubicles," says Mary Pierce, O+O's managing director. "We talked to standard manufacturers when we moved into the space, and they couldn't think outside the box."

ODI began its long search in 1994 for vendors that were willing to work with the unusual specifications. Pierce wanted low tables strong enough to hold monitors and comfortable lounge chairs with wide arms that looked tailored and professional. Finally two manufacturers were able to give ODO and O+O what they needed. They were High Point, NC-based Davis Furniture for the tables and Toronto-based Arconas for the chairs. Pierce says that today, many manufacturers are calling her for tours of the office so they can get a better idea of what kinds of products clients with AO environments need to support their work processes. In fact, that's the final word on AO furniture. Manufacturers are more willing now than ever to help you find the right solution to your AO requirements.

Now if they could only put castors on panel systems...

written by:
Marilyn Zelinsky *is the author of* New Workplaces for New Workstyles *(McGraw-Hill 1998), a reference work on alternative officing, and her forthcoming book:* The Practical Home Office: Real-Life Design & Lifestyle Dilemmas & Solutions *(McGraw-Hill). She is the former senior editor at* Interiors Magazine *and has written for several other national publications including* Home Office Computing Magazine. *She has reported extensively on product design, and is a specialist on the subject of alternative work environments. She is also a member of the National Telecommuting Advisory Council.*

[T . L . C .]

Tables Lovin' Chairs. Only at Versteel.

You knew us as Monsanto Contract Fibers.

WE ARE THE PEOPLE THAT IMPROVED NYLON 6,6.

WE ARE THE PEOPLE THAT BRING YOU THE UNSURPASSED COLORS OF ULTRON® VIP.

WE ARE THE PEOPLE STANDING AT THE TECHNOLOGICAL FOREFRONT.

LEADING A BRAND NEW COMPANY WITH 96 YEARS OF EXPERIENCE.

WE ARE NOW STRONGER. MORE FOCUSED. MORE AGILE.

WE ARE SOLUTIA.

AT SOLUTIA, WE ARE DESIGNING THE FUTURE. COME WITH US.

The
New York
Design
Center

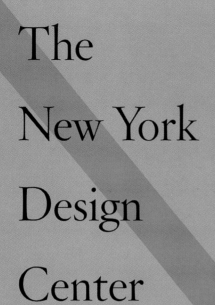

NY
DC

200

Lexington

Avenue

Taste, elegance,

and style

for interiors

since 1926

Nima™
CORNFIELD II
IN BRONZE TONES
SHOWN.
ALSO AVAILABLE
IN KHAKI/KHAKI
AND RUST/YELLOW.
STANDARD SIZES
5.6' X 8' TO 10' X 14'.
CUSTOM SIZES
TO 20' X 28'.

YACHT CLUB
IN HEMP, SAGE AND
TAUPE SHOWN.
CUSTOM COLORS
AND SIZES, WITH
3 MONTH DELIVERY.
HAND-TUFTED IN
GREECE IN
WOOL AND SILK
BY LILIA MÈLISSA
FOR ODEGARD.

COURT
IN GOLD SHOWN.
ALSO AVAILABLE
IN PLATINUM.
CUSTOM COLORS
AND SIZES, WITH
3 MONTH DELIVERY.
HAND-TUFTED IN
GREECE IN
WOOL AND SILK
BY LILIA MÈLISSA
FOR ODEGARD.

Nima™
ECLIPSE
IN MARIGOLD
SHOWN.
ALSO AVAILABLE
IN TOMATO,
MARINE BLUE,
YELLOW AND
TAUPE.
STANDARD SIZES
4' X 6' TO 10' X 14'.
CUSTOM SIZES
AND RUNNERS TO
20' X 28'.

© 1998 ODEGARD, INC.

AFTER ALL, ORIGINALITY IS WHAT INTERIOR DESIGN IS ALL ABOUT.

ORIGINAL HANDKNOTTED AND HANDTUFTED RUGS. EXCLUSIVE DESIGNS IN THE FINEST MATERIALS
AND PUREST COLORS. ANYTHING LESS IS EXACTLY THAT.

ODEGARD
Rare & Original Tibetan Carpets

THE NEW YORK DESIGN CENTER 200 LEXINGTON AVENUE, SUITE 1206 PHONE 212 545-0069 FAX 212 545-0298
THE WASHINGTON DESIGN CENTER 300 D STREET SW SPACE 322 PHONE 202 484-5888 FAX 202 484-6077

LUCEPLAN
USA

TITANIA
1989

TRAMA
1986

BERENICE
1985

COSTANZA
1986

LOLA
1987

**The LUCEPLAN
Lighting Collection**

Distinctive forms providing fine
illumination for interior spaces.

Grace of movement and great
attention to detail characterize
these award-winning products
designed in Italy and found
internationally in many museum
design collections.

Now readily available in the USA,
please call 1-800-268-7790 for
further information.

LUCE
PLAN USA

315 Hudson Street New York NY 10013 Tel 212-989-6265 Fax 212-462-4349

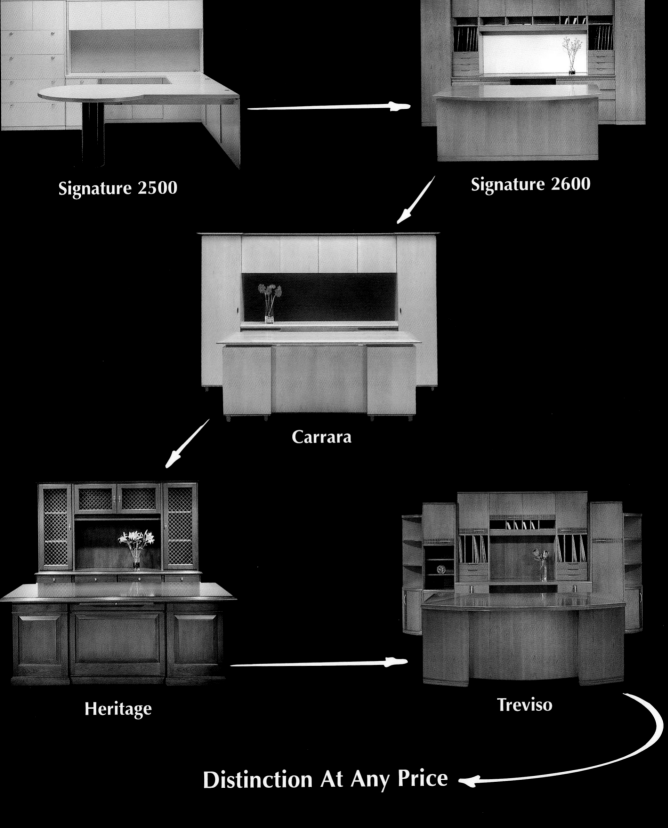

Signature 2500

Signature 2600

Carrara

Heritage

Treviso

Distinction At Any Price

GIANNI

SAHCO
HESSLEIN

BERGAMO
FABRICS

HARDEN contract

THE
GATSBY
COLLECTION

Designed by John Stafford

8550 Mill Pond Way • McConnellsville, New York 13401

315-675-3600 • Fax 315 / 245-2284

E-Mail: contract@harden.com • WebSite: http://www.furniture-office.com

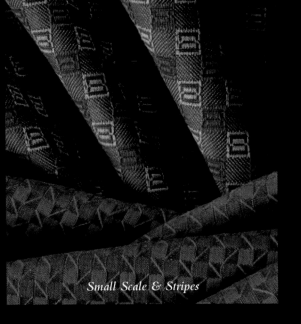

Small Scale & Stripes

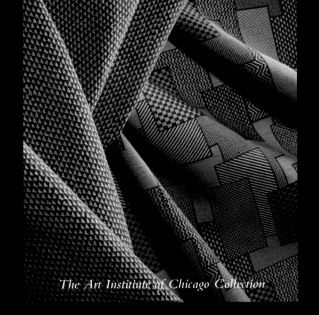

The Art Institute of Chicago Collection

CLASSICS FOR THE CORPORATE MARKET

The 3 x 5 Collection

Chromatique

SCHUMACHER.
CONTRACT

circe design by Renato Toso and Noti Massari

T 19/L

S 35

S 19

CIRCE
Bringing
Artistry
to Light

LEUCOS® *LIGHTING*

LEUCOS USA, inc.
70 Campus Plaza II, Edison, NJ 08837

tel 732 .225.0010 fax 732 .225.0250

|m|a|h|a|r|a|m|

Tek-Wall®

Tek-Wall® Naturals 40 woven wallcoverings with natural fiber texture and Tek-Wall® performance.

800.645.3943

INDEX BY PROJECTS

INDEX OF ADVERTISERS